THE REMNANT CHURCH

By

Rev. Msgr. Richard L. Carroll

THE AUTHOR

Rev. Msgr. Richard L. Carroll, Pastor of St. Margaret Mary, Slidell, Louisiana, since January 17, 1970. He is the author of *A Priest Looks At Medjugorje*. His brother Rev. Msgr. Ralph Carroll is Pastor of St. Clement of Rome in Metairie, Louisiana. They have a sister, Yvonne Hymel. Their parents are Ralph Carroll and the late Myrlie Gremillion Carroll.

FIRST EDITION
First Printing - 4,000
Second Printing - 10,000

REVISED EDITION

All rights reserved, including the right of reproduction in whole or in part in any form.

Copyright @ 1993 by Rev. Msgr. Richard L. Carroll

Printed by Book Crafters
Chelsea, Michigan

Manufactured in the United States of America
ISBN: 0-9643572-0-8

Library of Congress Catalog Card No: Pending

For additional copies: St. Margaret Mary Church
The Remnant Church
1050 Robert Blvd.
Slidell, Louisiana. 70458
504-643-6124
Fax. 504-643-6126

TABLE OF CONTENTS

CHAPTER	TITLE	PAGE

INTRODUCTION iii

ACKNOWLEDGEMENTS vi

Chapter 1 A EUCHARISTIC COMMUNITY ... 1

Chapter 2 A MARIAN COMMUNITY 12

Chapter 3 A SUFFERING COMMUNITY 32

Chapter 4 PRAYERFUL CHILDREN 50

Chapter 5 THE ARK 55

Chapter 6 EVANGELIZATION 67

Chapter 7 SATAN THE REAL ENEMY 85

Chapter 8 LOYALTY TO THE POPE-THE
           THE LITMUS TEST 96

Chapter 9 TOTAL CONSECRATION TO JESUS
           THROUGH MARY.................................104

Chapter 10 VISIT TO DENVER 112

Chapter 11 SPIRIT FILLED COMMUNITY ..124

Chapter 12 THE ANGEL OF TRIUMPH 130

Chapter 13 FATIMA - A LINK TO
           THE FUTURE 138

Chapter 14 THE KEYS TO THE TRIUMPH OF
           THE IMMACULATE HEART 152

Chapter 15 DIVINE MERCY................................. 177

ENTRUSTMENT

This small work is entrusted to Mary the Mother of Jesus. The Council of Ephesus in 430 AD also called her the Mother of God. I have come to know her as my Mother. It is to her that I humbly dedicate this work to be used by her as she wishes. To Jesus through Mary!

INTRODUCTION

The Remnant Church is a journal of one Catholic Community, St. Margaret Mary Parish, Slidell, Louisiana. The Holy Spirit has led many in the community, priests and parishioners to try to live the gospel messages of penance, prayer, love for Jesus through the Eucharist and devotion to our Blessed Mother.

This is a journal of the spiritual growth of a parish. It is the story of an entire community seeking to make Jesus the Lord of our lives. The Holy Spirit isn't finished with us yet. But it is our hope that our story may inspire you to be open to the work of the Holy Spirit in your community.

In an unprecedented way, our Blessed Mother is revealing herself today throughout the world to visionaries. The great Marian scholar, Father Rene Laurentin in the second edition of a newspaper entitled *Queen of Peace*, distributed by the Pittsburgh Center for Peace said: "the ultimate aim of apparitions is not to complete the faith by objective information, but to renovate and stimulate it. In that sense it pertains more to hope than faith. Their function (apparitions) is to regulate conduct and plan the future rather than unveiling truths. Father Laurentin posed a question: Medjugorje is the Fatima of our days. The hours of the apparitions follow a progression. At Lourdes they took place in the morning. At Fatima at noon. At Medjugorje, in the evening. Is it the end of a long day and the announcement of the eighth day?"

This may help explain my reason for quoting visionaries from Medjugorje, Yugoslavia; Akita, Japan; Co Mayo, Ireland; Fatima, Portugal and Garabandal, Spain. I feel our Lady is trying to warn us that the time of tribulation may be at our doorstep. Repentance is a message repeated by our Lady through all of these visionaries. A time of tribulation is expected prior to an era of peace predicted by Our Lady. Is this time of tribulation happening now?

St. Paul in 2 Thessalonians 2:9-12(1) explains the importance of relying on the judgment of Holy Mother, the Church, and the Holy Father, the Pope in particular. St. Paul tells us, "this lawless one will appear as part of the workings of Satan, accompanied by all the power and signs and wonders at the disposal of falsehood -- by every seduction the wicked can devise for those destined to ruin because they have not opened their hearts to the truth in order to be saved. Therefore God is sending upon them a perverse spirit which leads them to give credence to falsehood, so that all who have not believed the truth but have delighted in evil doing will be condemned."

Therefore, it is important to know that the Catholic Church is the final judge of the authenticity of private revelations. There are Marian scholars who believe that the apparitions of Our Blessed Mother at Medjugorje and Christina Gallagher are authentic. The Catholic Church has not yet passed judgment on them. Since loyalty to the teaching authority of the Church, and in particular the Pope, are a key element to the REMNANT CHURCH, I pledge my adherence to that final decision.

By the Decree of the Congregation for the Doctrine of the Faith, approved by Pope Paul VI on October 14, 1966 and which came into effect on March 29, 1967, Canon 1399 was abrogated. Also suppressed was Canon 2318. The new code does not contain these canons. Since then, it is permitted to publish texts referring to alleged revelation, apparitions, prophecies, or miracles without engaging the Holy Roman Catholic Church, provided that the writer willingly submits himself to the ultimate official pronouncement of the Church on the matter and provided the content of the messages or revelations does not constitute danger to the faith or morals of the faithful. This book is published on that basis. An Imprimatur has not been sought, as the events recorded are under examination.

****

I believe our Blessed Mother is calling you for help to form the Remnant Church. Jesus himself warned us: When the Son of Man comes will He find any faith at all? I will share with you some of the pieces of the puzzle to becoming part of the Remnant Church; it will be Eucharistic, Marian, Prayerful and Suffering, Loyal to the Holy Father and truly Spirit filled. Perhaps there are others that we are yet to learn. Our Lady wants every Catholic Parish to be part of the Remnant Church. This may involve persecution. May each of you play a major role in the Triumph of the Immaculate Heart of Mary. The prophecies of Fatima may be fulfilled in our lifetime, Russia will be converted and world Peace will occur.

In the first edition of The Remnant Church, we included alleged apparitions by Theresa Lopez.

On March 9, 1994, Archbishop Stafford of Denver, decided these apparitions are not trustworthy. The Archbishop wrote, "as Archbishop of Denver, I have concluded that the alleged apparitions of the Blessed Virgin Mary to Theresa Antonia Lopez are devoid of any supernatural origin."(2)

Despite the fact that Theresa Lopez, is a very sincere individual we must listen to our Bishops who are in union with Rome.

I have therefore deleted all mention of Theresa from the Revised Edition.

ACKNOWLEDGMENTS

This book is the spiritual journey of an entire community. St. Margaret Mary parish is located in Slidell, Louisiana in the Archdiocese of New Orleans.

I am particularly grateful to those who have shared intimate details of their journey with you. I am sure that they will be richly rewarded for their willingness to surrender to Jesus through Mary by sharing the gifts they have been given. Many spiritual gifts are given for the benefit of the community as well as the individual.

I would like to acknowledge my wonderful staff in the church, school and C.C.D. offices. In a special way, I would like to recognize Joleen Megilligan, Alice Sanders, Shannon Megilligan and Linda Latour. In addition to implementing my dreams and that of our community, these key lay personnel have spent countless hours working on this manuscript. Special thanks are due to Alan and Rosemary Fries, Kim Allabaugh, Veralyn Alpha, Beverly Fisher, Imelda Besh, Pat Dalton, Patsie Meyer and others for editing this book.

I also felt the personal testimony of Father Mossy Gallagher, Father Ken Harney and Father Joseph Benson enriched this journal.

ABOUT THE COVER

The front cover is a picture of St. Margaret Mary Church. It is printed on black stock to convey the feeling that each part of the Remnant Church will be a bright light in a dark world. It will stand out for all to see. It reminds us of the injunction of Christ, Let your light shine before men.

The stained glass window was executed by Milton Pounds, a local artist from Covington, Louisiana. The idea that I asked him to convey was the centrality of the Cross. It is only by the Cross of Jesus that we are saved. It is the Cross that tells of an immeasurable love that Jesus has for each of us. Greater love than this no man has, that He lay down his life for his friends.

Inside the Cross is a picture of the Host representing the Eucharist. To be part of the Remnant Church there must be acceptance of the words of Jesus, "he who feeds on my flesh and drinks my blood has life eternal and I will raise him up on the last day." The Gospel of John 6:54.

The colors of red and gold are a reminder of a sign seen by many in Medjugorje. The cross on top of the hill changes colors from red to gold. Jesus is trying to get our attention through his Mother.

[1]Please Note: All Biblical quotations in this book come from *The New American Bible*.

[2]Letter from Archbishop J. Francis Stafford. Declaration concerning alleged apparitions of the Blessed Virgin Mary at Mother Cabrini Shrine and Other Places in the Archdiocese of Denver.

Chapter 1
A EUCHARISTIC COMMUNITY

"He who feeds on my flesh and drinks my blood has eternal life and I will raise him up at the last day."
The Gospel of John 6:54.

It must sadden the heart of our Lord Jesus at the indifference of so many Catholics. Constantly, Our Lady has urged us to make the Mass the central act of our life. I believe one of the trials during the purification will center on the Mass and the Eucharist - the denial of the Real Presence.

As I read the sad statistics in the National Catholic Reporter that only 30% believe what the church teaches on the Real Presence of Christ, my mind went back to an earlier heresy - The Protestant Revolt. It was not the so called "selling of indulgences" that caused the painful break in our family. It was bishops and priests who no longer believed in the Real Presence. Will Durant wrote in *The History of Civilization,* "Petrarch lamented the fact that in the minds of many scholars it was a sign of ignorance to prefer the Christian religion to pagan philosophy. In Venice (1530), it was found that most of the upper ranks neglected their Easter Duties. Luther claimed to have found a saying current among the educated classes in Italy on going to Mass; 'Come let us conform to the popular error'...Erasmus was astonished to find that at Rome, the fundamentals of the Christian faith were topics of skeptical discussion among the Cardinals. One ecclesiastic undertook to explain to him the absurdity of belief in a future life, others smiled at Christ and the Apostles. Many, he assures us, claimed to have heard papal functionaries blaspheming the Mass. The lower class kept their faith as we shall see. The thousands who heard Savonarola must have believed, but the soul of the great Creed has been pierced with the arrows of doubt."(1)

If you are to be a Remnant Church, you must have the childlike faith of a seven year old. The value of the Mass comes from the fact that Jesus, the Son of God, using a human instrument, a Catholic priest, offers himself in an unbloody sacrifice or gift to God the Father. It is Jesus offering Himself to the Father that makes the sacrifice of the Mass an unbelievable treasure to us as Catholics. In a sacramental way, it puts us in the upper room when He changed bread and wine to His Body and Blood. It also puts us at His feet on the cross.

The Mass is not only a SACRIFICE, IT IS A SACRAMENT. It is through the Mass that we receive the Body and Blood of Jesus Christ. With all our hearts, St. Margaret Mary community believes this truth. It is truly Jesus that we receive in Holy Communion! Jesus promised in the Gospel of John 6:54 *"He who feeds on My flesh and drinks My blood has life eternal."* Only one gifted as a child can accept Jesus at His word.

When Catholics are asked, "Do you have a personal relationship with Jesus Christ?" they should answer a resounding YES! There is no closer union with Jesus than when you receive Him in the Eucharist. You too can say with St. Paul, "... and the life I live now is not my own; CHRIST IS LIVING IN ME." Galatians 2:20

Jesus made the Eucharist the litmus teSt. "... If you do not eat the flesh of the Son of Man and drink His blood, you have no life in you." The Gospel of John 6:53.

When asked if you have a relationship with

Jesus Christ you should say, "Because of His grace, Jesus is truly my Lord. I have an intimate relationship with Him. I receive Him daily in Holy Communion."

Finally, Adoration of the Blessed Sacrament is a sign of a community that is truly Eucharistic. Since 1983, I have asked our parishioners to spend one hour a week in prayer before the Blessed Sacrament. Many of them have responded and have grown into a deep prayer life. Countless families have been touched and many of our youth are now powerful prayer partners in the battle against Satan. But there are many of them who are too busy. They have centered their lives on trifles.

As we have many parishioners who move out of Slidell each year, it is necessary to attract new members to Perpetual Adoration. The question that I pose to our congregation is the same that Jesus asked Peter, James and John in the Garden of Gethsemane, "Can you not watch and pray for one hour?" The time of testing is upon us. Tomorrow may be too late!

I have a sense of joy about our parish, St. Margaret Mary. I believe Our Lady is forming us. The only thing we need fear is sin itself. I believe all of us will live to see marvelous signs and wonders if only we do our part to make the remnant community. As a Father, my only desire in life is to see my parishioners reaping the rewards of God's glory because of their fidelity. I know they will choose to accept Our lady's invitation to become a **REMNANT COMMUNITY**.

A REMNANT COMMUNITY

One Saturday Morning as I sat in the chapel at

2:00 a.m., I asked for the inspiration to put into words an important message which I feel you need to hear if you are to be a remnant community.

I believe that the Holy Spirit is leading our community through the powerful prayers of our children to be offered a challenge and a great task, and perhaps a great trial. I feel we are being called to become one of the great lights in a darkened world. Normally, because I have always been an individual mired in fear, I would not have acted as their spokesman and would have told that I am not up to the task.

It will be a high risk. Some will feel that we are going over the edge. Many individuals today are only interested in a "feel good" theology. The warnings of Our Lady at Medjugorje seem to go unheeded. But we must accept the invitation. We must become a remnant community.

The Holy Spirit has gifted this community in extraordinary ways since 1983, when they began to spend an hour each week in Perpetual Adoration. The gifts of the Holy Spirit abound.

In 1991 Josyp Terelya, a visionary from the Ukraine, spoke at St. Margaret Mary Church. He shared the struggle of being jailed for more than 20 years for the crime of being Catholic. He told of the joy of seeing our Blessed Mother twice while in jail and later in Hrushu, after he was freed.

It was Josyp Terelya who first told us face to face that the time of testing found in the Book of Revelation is now upon us. This same message echoed in the interlocutions of Father Gobbi on many occasions.

The Holy Spirit is molding many of our youth

in Peer Ministry. I have witnessed their empowerment by the Holy Spirit. Some of them actually saw Our Lady; many others felt her presence in their lives. What else would explain the many hours they have labored in retreats and prayer groups and countless meetings to give back to Mary some of the love she lavished on her choice brood.

DIVINE MERCY

There is a basic need for Divine Mercy if we are truly to be a Eucharistic community. As this community has grown in the workings of the Holy Spirit, we have come to accept the fact that each of us is a sinner, and we need the mercy of Jesus Christ. The late Bishop Sheen wrote: "I thank God I am a sinner, now I can have Jesus Christ as my Savior."(2)

Sister Faustina was another piece of the puzzle we had to discover. Our Lord Jesus Christ made a very special promise to Sister Faustina. Jesus requested that the church establish a Feast of Divine Mercy honoring Him in a very special way. Christ told Sister Faustina, "It is my desire that it be solemnly celebrated on the first Sunday after Easter. I desire that the Feast of Mercy be refuge and shelter for all souls and especially for poor sinners. On that day, the very depths of My tender mercy is open. I pour out a whole ocean of graces upon those souls who approach the fount of mercy."

Jesus went on to tell Sister Faustina, "The soul that will go to confession (within 8 days before or after Mercy Sunday) and receives Holy Communion shall obtain complete forgiveness of sins and punishment. Let no soul fear to draw near to Me even though its sins be as scarlet."(3)

To be a remnant community we must be

witness to the mercy of Jesus Christ. To truly be a Eucharistic community we must do more than believe in the Real Presence of Christ in the Eucharist, or even to spend time in Perpetual Adoration. We must see ourselves as sinners...and in need of Divine Mercy.

Mrs. Christina Gallagher, a visionary from Ireland, told of seeing two angels: one was in white and the other was in red. She was told that 1992 is a critical year. The white angel represents God's love and mercy; the red represents God's justice.(4) If this is true, the final hours for the outpouring of Jesus' mercy, which He predicted to Sister Faustina, are upon us. We must accept the challenge to be a Remnant Church.

We can become the Remnant Church that Jesus wants. First we must become a Eucharistic community. We must accept the teaching of Christ that the Eucharist is the Body and Blood of Christ which we receive. It is Jesus we receive in the Communion. But we must also acknowledge that we are sinners and learn to rely on the mercy of Jesus Christ, who is our Lord and Savior.

HOW JESUS BECAME LORD OF OUR PARISH

Frequently, visitors will stop after Mass and comment about St. Margaret Mary Community. "I don't know what it is," they say, "but there is something different about this parish." Usually I accept the compliment graciously, knowing that all the glory belongs to the Holy Spirit because this community is different. It all happened when Jesus became Lord of our lives through Perpetual Adoration.

Father Martin Lucia, S.S. C.C.

The change began in 1983. It was a sermon that would affect all of us. Father Martin Lucia, S.S. C.C. preached at every Mass on December 16, 1983. He told the people the great blessings that would come to Slidell if they would agree to spend one hour of adoration before the Blessed Sacrament. If a large enough number would volunteer to spend time in the chapel in prayer, we would keep the chapel open night and day. This is called "Perpetual Adoration."

The theological basis for adoration of the Eucharist is the belief that Jesus Christ is truly present in both the consecrated bread and consecrated wine. The Catholic Church teaches that after the consecration of the Mass, the elements of bread and wine truly become "the Body and Blood of Christ." The Council of Trent in the 16th century defined: "The body and the blood of Christ, together with his soul and divinity, therefore, the whole Christ, is truly present in the Eucharist." The promise Jesus gave us in John 6 of His Flesh and Blood were fulfilled at the Last Supper. When Jesus told the apostles to "do this in remembrance of me;" we have continued to follow this injunction.

Traditionally, the Church has reserved the leftover consecrated hosts in a tabernacle. This allows the priest to administer communion to the sick and dying at any time night or day. It also allows Catholics a focus. Christ is present among us in every tabernacle. As He promised, He did not leave us orphans.

To the amazement of many, a large number of individuals signed up to spend an hour in prayer. Since that first night following the 7:00 p.m. Mass, the chapel has not been closed. Every hour night and day, someone is there adoring Jesus present in the Eucharist.

The results have been amazing. The number of adult converts dramatically increased. The prayer life of the people deepened. Miracles of grace occurred.

One small example will suffice. A young teen wrote in the Book of Intentions in the chapel, "I intend to kill myself, I have nothing to live for." A few days later, there was another note. "I changed my mind after praying before the Blessed Sacrament. I have given my life over to Jesus Christ. Everything will work out."

The public praise at the Sunday liturgies has taken on a character of joy. There is an excitement of knowing that they belong to Jesus Christ. Despite the turmoil of the world, there is a sense of inner peace as soon as you enter the church.

The huge window that was erected in the entrance of St. Margaret Mary Church, which is pictured on the front of this book is a visual representation of our community. The **CROSS** is a sign that Jesus is our Lord and Savior. We are all aware that it is through the cross of Jesus that our salvation is assured.

The **WHITE HOST** in the center of the cross is a reminder that the **EUCHARIST IS THE BODY AND BLOOD OF CHRISt.** This is a core teaching of Jesus. Jesus is still present among us in the Eucharist. When we receive Holy Communion, we are receiving Jesus. It is a mystery of Divine Love.

When we are asked if we are saved, as Catholics we can say with the strongest evangelical, "Through the power of the cross and the acceptance of Jesus as Lord and the grace of the Holy Spirit, we will be saved." But as Catholics, we also have the assurance of Jesus, "He who feeds on my flesh and drinks my blood has eternal life, and I will raise him up on the last day." The Gospel of John 6:54

Jesus became Lord of our lives when we as a community took Him at His word. He said He would give us His Body and Blood as food and drink. When we proved our belief in the Real Presence by spending 24 hours a day, seven days a week in adoration, He allowed the Holy Spirit to change us. Now each of us can say to Jesus the same words that Pope John Paul II loves to use, "Totus Tuus" ... "Totally Yours." We are totally yours, Lord Jesus Christ. For Jesus is Lord of our community because He is the Lord of our lives.

Sister Briege McKenna shared a story about a major seminary in this country. The spiritual director decided that in place of his weekly talk, the students would spend an hour before the Blessed Sacrament. The major seminarians protested; "We are not bread watchers." One of the trials that will afflict this country will be that of schism, the denial of basic Catholic teaching. There is no teaching more integral to our faith as Catholics than belief in the Real Presence of Christ in the Eucharist.

One of our peer ministers, Christine, told us a beautiful story. She spent some time in Yugoslavia and became friends with Marija, one of the visionaries from Medjugorje. One day as the two young women were together, Christine asked Marija a question; "Is the story about the Eucharist true?"

A few months before, Marija was recovering

from surgery. Our Blessed Mother appeared to the young visionary. "Marija, get up and get ready," Our Lady urged, "Jesus is coming to visit you." Our Blessed Mother helped the young woman pick out her best dress and assisted her as she prepared herself for the visit of Jesus. As soon as she was dressed Our Lady left her. Marija answered a knock on the door. It was one of the priests coming to bring her Holy Communion.

"Well is it true?" Christine begged.

"Of course it is true," Marija responded. "She is such a mother!"

Every Catholic parish is called to be a Remnant Church. It begins with a childlike belief in the Real Presence of Christ in the Eucharist. We are all unworthy, we are all sinners. But do you truly believe it is Jesus that you receive in Holy Communion? Or are you like those students studying to be priests who would not spend an hour in adoration before the Blessed Sacrament? The remnant communities will truly be Eucharistic! In order to receive this grace we must accept the Divine Mercy of Jesus Christ. We are sinners, but we have Jesus as our Savior!

[1]Will and Ariel Durant, *Story of Civilization* (New York: Simon & Schuster, 1967).

[2]Speech of Bishop Sheen in English, other information unknown.

[3]Sister M. Faustina Kowalska, *Divine Mercy in My Soul: Diary* (Stockbridge, Massachusetts: Marian Press, 1987).

[4]R. Vincent, *Please Come Back To Me And My Son: Our Lady's Appeal Through Christina Gallagher* (Westmeath, N. Ireland: Ireland's Eye Publications, 1992).

Chapter 2
A MARIAN COMMUNITY

"... All ages to come shall call Me blessed."
The Gospel of Luke 1:48.

In the Old Testament, Jeremiah prophesied about the "Day of the Lord" which in the Bible is a time of great trial, similar to our own. Jeremiah writes, "woe to the shepherds who mislead and scatter the flock of my pasture, says the Lord. Therefore, thus says the Lord, the God of Israel, against the shepherds who shepherd my people: 'You have scattered my sheep and driven them away. You have not cared for them, but I will take care to punish your evil deeds. I myself will gather the remnant of my flock from all the lands to which I have driven them and bring them back to their meadow; there they shall increase and multiply. I will appoint shepherds for them who will shepherd them so that they need no longer fear and tremble; and none shall be missing,' says the Lord."
Jeremiah 23:1-4

I believe that the Holy Spirit is leading this community, through the powerful prayers of our children, to accept the challenge to become one of the great lights of the church in a darkened world. I believe we must accept the offer of Our Lady to become a remnant community.

Since 1983 when we began to spend an hour each week in Perpetual Adoration, the Holy Spirit has gifted this community in extraordinary ways. The culmination of many of the gifts given to us are now at hand.

It was Josyp Terelya, a visionary from Russia, who first told us face to face that the time of testing, found in the Book of Revelation, is now upon us. On many occasions the same message is echoed in the interlocutions of Father Gobbi.

Our Lady has led me to consecrate the St. Margaret Mary school children to the Sacred Heart of Jesus and the Immaculate Heart of Mary. I believe this is one of the pieces of the puzzle that will help prepare our community for the time of testing.

I was confronted with a difficult task when I had to speak to the school children concerning fear. One of the eighth grade students had brought a handgun to the campus after school at a fish fry. Out of fear, many of the children hid his secret. It could have been a disaster. No one was hurt because the janitor discovered the gun before it was accidentally discharged.

The janitor told me that as a young man he had brought a gun into a bar. When he was confronted by another patron, he pulled the gun out and shot it at the man's head. Fortunately for him, the gun did not discharge. From that moment, he turned his life over to Jesus Christ.

But could this story from Sam, the janitor, help me to teach the students to confront fear in the future? Somehow, I knew the answer was CONSECRATION. All of the children should be consecrated to the Sacred Heart of Jesus and the Immaculate Heart of Mary. The following talk was given in April, 1992.

Consecration of St. Margaret Mary School Children to the Sacred Heart of Jesus and the Immaculate Heart of Mary

My dear children,

This morning I am going to consecrate each and every one of you, your classrooms, gym, cafeteria, library, and administration building to the Sacred Heart of Jesus and the Immaculate Heart of Mary. I ask our principal, teachers, administrators, coaches, cafeteria staff, and parents to join the children in making St. Margaret Mary truly Holy Ground by our consecration to the Sacred Heart of Jesus and the Immaculate Heart of Mary.

The reason that we make this consecration today is to put ourselves totally under the care, protection, comfort, support and love of the Sacred Heart of Jesus and the Immaculate Heart of Mary. We pray that the Holy Spirit will cast out every fear from our hearts; that He might give us the courage never to give in to fear or anxiety because we know we belong to Jesus and His mother, Mary, who is also our Mother.

I have shared with you, my children, the terrible fear I experienced as a child in a Catholic school. I was beaten up by bullies because I was too small. I was embarrassed because I was seen to be weak. I was ashamed because I was shy, and fear reigned in my heart as a little one.

I promised my Blessed Mother that I would try never to allow fear, shame, or embarrassment to grieve one of my children because of my neglect. Fear has no place in a Catholic school which is sacred ground.

There is no doubt in my mind that the Holy Spirit intends to use each and every one of us in a very powerful way...provided we learn together what the Holy Scripture teaches: "perfect love casts out fear". By the Blood of Jesus Christ shed on the cross, I rebuke Satan, the prince of fear, in each of you. May the love of Jesus replace any worry or anxiety in your lives.

My dear children, the Holy Spirit has taught me, once a frightened little child, that the Satan of fear cannot touch you as long as you are consecrated to the Sacred Heart of Jesus and the Immaculate Heart of Mary. The love of Jesus and His precious mother will fill your heart with love as fear is dispelled.

I began to write Thursday morning at midnight. For just a moment, I imagined a little of the pain that must have been in the heart of Jesus as He suffered in the Garden of Gethsemane. I thought my heart would split in two. I felt this hurt because I knew that when I would speak to you today, one of my sons would not be here to listen. I knew one of my special children would never graduate from our school because of the serious offense of bringing a gun on school property last Friday evening. This could have caused serious harm, even loss of life to himself or one of my precious little ones. Yet, I also knew he was not here today because he did not learn how to overcome fear. People who carry guns are either criminals or frightened people. He is not a criminal...he is a frightened young person.

For my failure to teach him to overcome fear, I ask pardon of God and forgiveness from each and every one of you. I also realize I have failed those who allowed themselves to be negatively influenced (bullied) by this child or any other child in this school. I ask your pardon and your forgiveness.

I also failed those who, if they had been taught manly Christian courage by me, would have prevented this from ever occurring, those who lacked courage including the child who helped him buy a gun, those who attempted to help him get rid of the gun, and those who knew about the gun but did nothing about it. For all of these accomplices to the crime of fear and the lack of courage, I beg pardon from you, my children, that I failed to teach them courage.

I know our Blessed Mother is not angry with you or even the student who is no longer here. I believe Mary is just sad that I failed so badly to teach you to overcome fear and put on the armor of Jesus Christ.

The day has come when you must stand up to fear with courage. The only thing that can truly hurt you is sin. Our Blessed Mother has taught me that Satan tries to scare us, but he can't touch us as long as we are under the protection of the Sacred Heart of Jesus and the Immaculate Heart of Mary. You also have a powerful guardian angel who stands watch over you night and day.

As I asked the Lord Jesus to guide me in what I should say to you today, I listened to a tape by Father Jozo, who was the Pastor in Medjugorje, Yugoslavia, when the apparitions began. Father Jozo explained how Our Blessed Mother had taught his children to overcome the evils of fear, hatred and anger. Many did not even speak to one another so bitter was their anger and the hurts of the paSt. One day in prayer, Our Lady told Father Jozo to teach the people to "Pray from their hearts". Father Jozo didn't understand what Mary meant by that.

"You can never pray from your heart," he was told, "as long as you have not forgiven one another." Father Jozo gathered the parish together, and they began to pray. "Grant us the gift to forgive," the priest pleaded to heaven; "For we can't pray from our hearts unless we forgive." For twenty minutes, there was nothing but silence. Father Jozo felt as if he was holding all of his people in his heart so burdened was he. Finally, a man with a deep voice cried out in the church: "Jesus, I forgive them, please forgive me." Torrents of tears were shed. Everyone in the church began to cry, "Jesus, I forgive them, please forgive me." Each began to sob out loud. Because of this gift of forgiveness that Jesus wanted from each of them, the whole community learned to pray from their hearts. That gift was given to each of them. Fear fled from their hearts.

This morning, my dear children, I will teach you the gift of surrender to God's will, the gift of courage and the gift of love. Simply pray that man's humble prayer, "Jesus, I forgive them, please forgive me." Forgiveness is the door to God's love.

For all the times I have failed you, I ask your pardon. I have loved each of you from the moment my eyes looked on you. I brought many of you into the church through the Sacrament of Baptism. I have given you the Body and Blood of Christ countless times. For those times I did not tell you I love you, for any hurts I have caused or allowed to happen to you, my children, I ask pardon.

If I, your spiritual Father, can ask for your forgiveness, I now ask you in your hearts to forgive any who may have hurt you and to ask forgiveness for any you may have injured. For any parents, principal, or teachers who hurt you, I ask that you pardon them. For any classmates, friends, acquaintances who caused you fear, anxiety, worry, I ask that you pardon them. For those who have bullied you or caused you pain, I ask you to forgive them. Simply say out loud, "Jesus, I forgive them, please forgive me."

My dear children, St. Paul tells us that perfect love casts out all fear. As we consecrate ourselves and our school to the Sacred Heart of Jesus and the Immaculate Heart of Mary after Mass, let us promise them that our love will overcome any problems or obstacles. We will not allow one child in the school to feel unloved. We will wrap our arms around each other and protect one another. Let it always be said of us: "See how they love one another."

The secret of casting out the Satan of fear is forgiving those who have injured us. It means loving even those who do not seem to love us. There is one other element. We must recognize that we are all "angels with only one wing". We ourselves are weak. By ourselves we cannot fly, but together we can soar like an eagle. We need to help each other. Put your one good wing together with your brother and sister and support one another.

Before she died, four year old Katie Hernandez promised to be your special angel. Whenever you are in need of help, ask Katie, your special angel, to protect you.

As I close, Mike Clavijo will sing a song, <u>Angel With Only One Wing.</u> While he is singing this song, I would ask you to hug two or three of your sisters and brothers including your teachers. For your love of each other will be your life long support.

After Mass we will bless your individual pictures of the Sacred Heart of Jesus and the Immaculate Heart of Mary. We will make the act of consecration and sing a final song. Each teacher will lead you to your classroom where you will install your picture in a prominent place.

Let the image of Jesus and Mary always remind you that perfect love will cast out all your fears. Remember each day to pray, "Jesus, I forgive them, forgive me too." And finally, know that this truly is Holy Ground because you have agreed to take care of your weak brothers and sisters and never consciously hurt or injure them. Try never to allow them to experience fear because of you or your actions or your neglect.

An artist has begun a huge window over the chapel entrance. It will be a picture of Our Blessed Mother overcoming the Satan of fear, who will be pictured as a snake. Under the picture of Mary you will see two small angels. One will remind you of Katie who is your special angel. The other will be an angel with only one wing. That angel stands for you and me. We are all wounded angels. By ourselves, we can never fly; but if we have the love and forgiveness of our sisters and brothers, we can soar to heaven.

THE BEGINNING OF A MARIAN COMMUNITY

How did it all begin? How did St. Margaret Mary Parish begin to be a remnant community? Clearly, Perpetual Adoration of the Blessed Sacrament was the first step. But devotion to Our Blessed Mother was a key element. It began in earnest after I returned from my sabbatical, August 1, 1987.

How Mary Changed My Life And Our Parish

In December, 1986, I received permission from Archbishop Hannan to take an eight month sabbatical. I had been a priest since 1959 and the pastor of St. Margaret Mary since 1970. The pain of dealing with the constant problems had taken its toll. I felt I could no longer cope as I should with the myriad of problems with which I was confronted. I was burned out!

In March of 1987 while I was on the sabbatical, I decided to visit the little town of Medjugorje in Yugoslavia. It had been reported since 1981, that Mary, the mother of Jesus, was appearing there daily to six children. Since I am skeptical by nature, I wanted to see for myself whether this was true.

On March 25 I was allowed to be in the place of apparition. At that time, it was occurring in a back room of the rectory. It was a very small room and there were few present. I went to the back of the room and stood quietly. Marija and Jakov, two visionaries, entered that day. They knelt and began to pray the Rosary. We all joined in our own language.

During the few minutes the apparition occurred, a strange phenomenon took place. I began to cry; I wept like I had not cried since my mother died. It was as if the Holy Spirit was washing away the hurts of the paSt. Once again I was that little child who loved Jesus with his whole heart and had a very special relationship to His mother, Mary. I learned later that tears are a gift of the Holy Spirit.

A religious experience is hard to explain. In our relationship to Christ, just as in a marriage, we can go through three stages. Falling in love, disillusionment, and then intimacy. The hurts of the priesthood had allowed disillusionment to set into my life. I felt unloved by Jesus. Now through the power of the Holy Spirit, I felt bathed in His love. I knew if Mary, my mother, loved me then surely Jesus himself must love me. I learned in an instant that Mary has a special love for all priests - even a sinner like me. I also discovered her love for each of you even those outside the Church. She wants to bring you to Jesus just as once again she brought me to His Sacred Heart. My life will never be the same because I will never doubt the love of Jesus, the care of His mother and the power of the Holy Spirit.

I believe the major change in my parish occurred through the intercession of Mary. By touching my heart, she changed the shepherd of the community and that would affect the sheep. Mary brought this community closer to Jesus by teaching me to be open to the power of the Holy Spirit.

I know my Protestant brothers and sisters have problems with accepting Mary as an intercessor. You feel that you can go directly to Jesus, and I am sure you do. However, many of us Catholics are like little children. You remember when you were small, whenever you wanted something really bad, you asked your mother to ask Dad for you. Mary has done that for us since Jesus gave her to us as our Mother when He said to John from the cross "...There is you mother." The Gospel of John 19:27.

Soon after I returned from Medjugorje, it became clear to me that I had been given a special gift. I was in Galveston at the time I discovered this gift of the Holy Spirit early one morning. I am sure it was due to the intercession of Our Blessed Mother.

I had been praying about the problem of addictions. I had met with an expert on the subject of addiction to food and alcohol. I was convinced that love was the answer to overcome the power of addictions. At two in the morning, I awoke to see a small cross on the wall of my apartment. It was an incredible sign. The cross of Jesus is the cure for addictions. I recalled the words of Jesus in the Gospel of John 3:14, "Just as Moses lifted up the serpent in the desert, so must the Son of Man be lifted up, ..." It was Christ lifted up on the cross that can cure addictions. It is through prayer and penance that we take the cross as our own.

As a result of this and other events, the Holy Spirit made me open to the fact that religious phenomena are a common occurrence in the Church today - Protestant as well as Catholic.

When I returned in August, 1987, I was confronted by a parent who shared the story of three small children outside our chapel. They looked up into the sky to discover a cross. It was red, and it turned gold. The Holy Spirit was beginning to empower our people. The gift to be open to the power of the Holy Spirit was a present from Our Blessed Mother to me and our community.

Since August, 1987, I have been present at numerous occasions where the Holy Spirit has empowered His people. A number of our youth while on retreat in Florida saw Mary. The last three confirmation classes have been prayed over by me, Deacon John Weber and members of our Peer Ministry Team. We have seen most of these 17 and 18 year old teens slain in the spirit. They simply fall back in prayer - like a state of ecstasy.

Finally, Mary has gifted me with a special favor. As I have shared often with my community, the sacrifices of the priesthood was not the loss of companionship or the pleasure of sex, but that I always wanted my own little girls. Our Blessed

Mother has opened my eyes. All of the children in this community are my little girls, regardless of their ages. They, like the little boys, truly are mine. In each little girl I see something special of Mary. It may be her beautiful hair or her loving smile. It may be her joyful heart or gentle spirit. Every one of them reminds me of Mary, my mother and yours.

TESTIMONY OF YOUTH

One of the high school students came in to suggest that we establish a Peer Ministry group for high school and college age students. Our first official program was a retreat in Florida. It was during the Peer Ministry retreat in Florida, in the summer of 1989 that I began to realize that these children truly belong to me, as I belong to them.

Three of the young people peering into the early morning sky saw Our Blessed Mother. The group came to the condos and woke the adults. All of us went to see if we would experience this phenomena. Most of us could smell a fragrant odor of roses as we left the buildings. When we reached the beach, I looked into the sky, but I could not see Our Lady. However, there was a blue ring around the moon. We spent the next few minutes huddled under blankets praying the rosary.

When we returned to Slidell, the young people shared their experience with the Sunday night 7:00 p.m. Mass. It was an amazing sight to see young people witnessing to the entire community. I have included a few of their testimonies. It truly was a spirit filled time for our community. It is my hope to have you realize that the Holy Spirit is working in the church today as never before since the first Pentecost.

(Angela Wilt)

On the weekend of April 21 thirty-one of us went on a Peer Ministry retreat in Destin, Florida. There were eighteen young people on this retreat. We all experienced a lot, both individually and as a group. As we grew closer together, we also grew closer to Mary. As we felt her love we also felt a stronger need for devotion to her.

We want to share some of our experiences so that other people can be embraced by her love. The gift the Blessed Mother gave me was a VISION OF HER AND HER SON Jesus.

(Angela Besh)

I was a little hesitant when we left for Florida. I had no idea why God wanted me there. All I knew was that this group was a dream that I had been hiding in my heart for a long time. When I talked it over with Father Carroll, he suggested a retreat to Florida. It seemed like the perfect way to begin a successful group.

Saturday had the most impact on me. I saw others, as well as myself, opening the door to our hearts and letting our true selves shine. All of us began to take off our masks and let ourselves be seen and heard for who we are, not what we appear to be.

The peace we felt was indescribable. I have never been in a room with so many strangers and felt so comfortable in my life. However, not everything was perfect. I felt the more I began to open myself up the more vulnerable I became.

Many differences arose among our group. It seemed all we had gained was slipping away, but through it all the peace we felt inside never strayed. It was Sunday morning when I realized what was happening and why. The fact was our faith was being put to the teSt. The more good we did the more present evil became. When Angie shared her talk on friendship, it had an impact on all of us. She told us that all we had was each other and that we had to set aside our differences to do good for others. After all, that was why we were there. The true healing came when Deacon John told us to walk up to the ones we had hurt or had been hurt us and say, "I love you and I'm sorry if I ever hurt you." When we began to do this, we could feel the healing. On Saturday, the evil words and gossip had nicked and cut our souls like a knife, but our words of forgiveness healed our wounds. We felt embraced by not only God, but by each other as well. I think that the perfect gift Our Blessed Mother gave to me on this retreat was not only seeing some special signs like the light around the moon or the smell of roses, but the inner peace that I now have.

(Lori Mire)
While walking out to the beach from our condo on April 22 at about midnight, the Lord gave me, April, Angela and Katie a very special blessing which I would like to share with you tonight. It occurred right after our Saturday night session. We were all so hyped that we couldn't sleep, so we decided to walk out to the beach. When we got to the beach, we all went our separate ways. I was watching the waves roll in; I glanced up at the moon and at that moment I saw the moon light up in the sky. I continued watching and saw layers of the moon falling away almost as if it was shedding. After this stopped, there was a bright new glow around the moon, and in the middle I SAW THE VIRGIN Mary! The only way I can explain this sight to you is in one word and that is "peaceful".

My initial reaction was one of disbelief. I

thought my eyes were playing tricks on me because this could not happen to me because I had done nothing to deserve such a blessing.

I called out April's name because she was the closest person to me; and I wanted to see if she saw the same thing I saw, or if she saw anything at all. Without having to explain to her what I saw, her immediate reaction after hearing me call her name was, "I know Lori, isn't she beautiful?"

(Michelle Clavijo)

Eventually that night, everyone heard what Lori just said. I was touched by the look in their eyes. While holding their hands, I could feel the Holy Spirit in me through them. When everyone finally came together, we headed out to the beach to say the Rosary. Oh what a feeling at 2:30 in the morning saying the Rosary and receiving the precious gift of the Blessed Mother in our hearts. This feeling brought back memories of my Thanksgiving trip to Medjugorje. It goes to show you that the Holy Spirit can touch you wherever you are. The teenagers who attended this retreat are wonderful. Some teens think it's not cool to get this religious stuff, but I think it's real cool. I pray that more teens can get more involved in this parish. Trust me; you will enjoy it. It feels so good. I feel I have a special bond with the people in this group.

The gift that Our Blessed Mother gave me was the strength to realize that all things are possible and to never give up.

(Margaret McInerney)

On the trip to Florida, I made lot of new friends. We all became close and shared a lot. As a group, we each opened up a part of ourselves and shared it. Florida to me was special because I felt that I was surrounded by love. I went there not knowing what to expect, but what I saw and felt made me very happy and peaceful. The signs we saw on the last night we were there were only proof of the love we were sharing. I hope that we can make you feel as though you are part of this community and that you have the opportunity to share in this love. The gift that the Blessed Mother gave me was seeing her.

(Katie Dalton)

When I was on my retreat, I learned and experienced a lot; but the one thing I will always hold dear is the love I found in Father Carroll. Angie, Michelle, and I were fortunate enough to ride to Destin with Father, so we had the advantage of getting to know him better. He was so much fun and so easy to talk to. It was like riding to Florida with your family. He played games with us and even let us drive his *fine* car. He was always glad to have us around; and when we wanted to talk to him, he was always ready to listen. But it was so much more than that. He is filled with a beautiful love that he wants to share with each one of us. When we had our experience with Mary on the beach, he focused that for us so that we knew that the Blessed Mother was really with us. He sees the good in us and encourages us to see good in others and ourselves. He helped me see myself in a whole new light - Christ's light. He encourages us to share our experiences with our friends so we will all become Christian witnesses. Fr. Carroll has told us that he loves us and I have experienced this first hand. So I can stand here and tell you honestly that there is no one outside of your immediate family who loves you more than this beautiful man.

(Michael Clavijo)

Peer Ministry is a very self-fulfilling thing. The feeling about this particular group of teens is its strong sense of belonging that we all need. I have seen a change of heart in some of my friends and also received a special feeling from them. We actually ministered to each other.

Our weekend retreat was an experience, but you would have had to experience it for yourself to really feel and understand what we're going through. Every single person was touched in a special way, but our blessing was not too easy to achieve. We had to, for a moment, let ourselves go. We had our share of difficulties, but we worked them out together. The Lord brought us all closer together. With the help of our friends, we discovered some gifts that we never knew we had. I think we all could become a little more tough with ourselves.

Our Blessed Mother gave me the gift of an awesome sight of her beautiful blue glow around the moon and the sweet aroma of roses. But the most special gift that I received was that beautiful affirmation of our group through the love that bonds us all together. I think the greatest thing that we gained from our weekend was that sense of embracement. We were truly embraced by God, embraced by each other, our friends; embraced by love.

"Her Father's Eyes"

Our Blessed Mother has favored me with many gifts since my first of three trips to Medjugorje. On one trip we took a group of 62, mostly teens, who have a great love for Our Blessed Mother. Many individuals experienced unusual phenomena on that trip. All of us came away deeper in love with Mary.

When I returned from my sabbatical, I was asked by my sister to say Mass at her home for her prayer group. The women in her group asked if I would mind having a dialogue homily. The first question was the hardest..."Father, is it difficult to be a priest?", one of them asked? "Yes," I answered! "It's not the fact that we can't marry; I always wanted my own little girls," I said. The woman who asked the question began to cry. "I told my sixteen year old, I wished she would run away. All you wanted were your own little girls."

What Our Lady has done for me is to make me realize that all of the little girls in this community, all of the little boys as well are "my children". After the reception of the title "Monsignor" that I received a few years ago, I continue to use the title "Father." There is no title more special to me. As St. Paul said in 1 Corinthians 4:15, "Granted you have ten thousand guardians in Christ, you have only one father. It was I who begot you in Christ Jesus through my preaching of the gospel."

Our Blessed Mother has given me many signs of her affection but none more dramatic than the cure of Kelly. In the most difficult of times, it always seemed that God would place this child in my path when I was most in need of encouragement. She entered our parochial school when she was seven. There was never a time that I saw Kelly that she did not bless me with her beautiful smile.

Kelly grew up, finished high school with honors and entered college. She was both beautiful and quite intelligent. But one day, she made a serious mistake. Perhaps it was because her best friend's father shot himself to death. We will never know what her motive was, but Kelly attempted suicide. She inhaled four and a half hours of carbon monoxide. When she was rushed to the hospital, she was given little hope for survival.

I was called to the local hospital to anoint Kelly. I couldn't believe it. Of all the people I have ever known, this young woman was one of the most gifted and talented. She had so much to live for, yet her life hung by a thread.

Soon afterwards, Kelly was taken to Jo-Ellen Smith hospital, which is a considerable distance from Slidell. There is a hypoberic chamber in that hospital. It was hoped the hospital could help her. On a visit to Jo-Ellen hospital, I gave her mother a rosary blessed by Our Lady at Medjugorje. Kelly's mother prayed constantly. The center medal in the rosary turned to a gold color.

I remember thinking to myself on one of my visits that of all the children that have meant so much to me, I had never told Kelly that I loved her. I promised myself that if she would recover I would tell her how much I have loved her since she was a child.

It was decided to take Kelly off the respirator. She would be left in God's hands. On Christmas Eve, a nurse found that she did not have a pulse, and she was no longer breathing. "She's gone" she said.

At that moment Kelly, still in a coma, felt herself floating on a cloud. She heard a familiar voice. "Kelly, Kelly, it's me, Pat". She recognized the voice of her dead brother, Patrick, who had been killed in a car wreck.

"Kelly, it's not your time yet. You are needed, and one day you will do something very important," Patrick said. "By the way," he continued, "tell Paul

I love him too." Later, Kelly learned that as Paul, her older brother was praying for her, he realized how seldom we tell those we love how we feel. "I just wish I'd told Patrick I loved him before he died," Paul said to himself. From beyond the grave came an answer he too was loved by Patrick.

It wasn't long before this miracle was complete. Kelly walked out of the hospital without any brain damage or side effects. Her case has been written up in a medical journal. The first thing Kelly did when she returned to Slidell was to knock on the rectory. "I just came to tell you I love you," she said.

For the first time, I could tell her that I loved her. The gift that Our Blessed Mother gave to me was the cure of a child that was precious in my sight. In subsequent retreats usually one of the choir members sings a song that says it all... *My Father's Eyes,* by Amy Grant. If any child ever had her father's eyes, it is Kelly. She has always been precious to me.

I have learned that all the children in this community have their father's eyes. They have my eyes. The gift of knowing that I am loved by Mary and by all of my children was a present from Our Lady herself.

Our Blessed Mother has frequently asked the laity to pray for priests. May each of them realize that all the children young and old in their parish have THEIR FATHER'S EYES!

Chapter 3
A SUFFERING COMMUNITY

"He who will not take up his cross and come after me is not worthy of me."
The Gospel of Matthew 10:38.

"When people recognize the true value of the cross, they really recognize the love of God which alone heals souls and hearts."(1)

One of the elements of a Remnant Community is the presence of victim souls. St. Paul tells us that we must "make up what is lacking in the sufferings of Jesus Christ." We know that Paul did not mean that Jesus didn't suffer enough. He meant that our suffering is joined to the sufferings of Jesus. Suffering in the eyes of Jesus has value.

In an age that glorifies pleasure and comfort, the importance of a "victim soul" becomes even more important. For his own reasons, God chooses the weak to continue to confound the wise. He selects individuals to carry the burden of the cross as a reminder to us that all of life passes quickly.

TED BESH

Ted Besh was a pilot with Delta Airlines. He is married to a beautiful wife and has six precious children. The oldest child at the time of his accident was a senior in high school; the youngest was only six. Ted was called to be a "victim soul". The following is the personal testimony of Ted Besh.

On November 25, 1977, the day after Thanksgiving, I was severely injured. It was the end of a fine job as an airline pilot, and a major turning point in my life and that of my family.

The day before, we had celebrated the holiday with old friends who had introduced us way back in 1956. We spent the day recalling old times and letting two families get together for a feast.

Friday, I decided to go for a bicycle ride for exercise. I had gotten interested in that activity as a means of staying in shape for my flying job. I had gotten to the point I was riding long distances, so I set off on a 25 mile ride about 3:30 in the afternoon. I had second thoughts about it due to the overcast gray skies, but decided I would be back before it was too dark for safety. About 20 miles into the ride, just as I was reentering Slidell, I was struck from the rear by a van driven by an 18 year old intoxicated driver. He was completely out of control and was just barreling down the road in his van.

I was thrown quite some distance down the roadway and slid to a stop about 120 feet later. I recall flying through the air realizing I was in a precarious situation but relatively uninjured at the time. I suspected things were going to get worse. As I struck the road surface on landing, I went numb from the waist down and figured I had broken my back and injured my spinal cord. I was right. I had broken the T-12 vertebrate and had damaged the cord. I had no idea what the future held.

I was taken to Ochsner Hospital in New Orleans where the doctors hoped to operate and repair the break after a few days. That way, my body would settle down, swelling in the injured area would subside, and the surgery would be most effective in restoring whatever usage I would eventually have of my lower body.

I was more seriously injured than anyone

realized and emergency surgery had to be performed the next evening. My back was shattered and I was bleeding internally. The doctors did what they could and installed a pair of steel rods to strengthen the area.

A couple of days later, I was laying in a Stryker frame steel bed in intensive care, sort of relaxing under the effects of pain killing drugs. At first, this was rather enjoyable. But I began to wonder if there would be a problem with addiction. I found I was hallucinating, but I rather liked it. I would see scenes reminiscent of looking into the sky when I was on my back. Every two hours, the nurses would turn the frame over and I would be looking down. At those times, I would see scenes similar to those you see when looking down from a plane or from a high hill or things you would see when scuba diving and looking down at the sea floor. It was all very entertaining.

Once, I was face down and looking into what appeared to be an old-fashioned well found on many farms fifty or so years ago. The well appeared to be about five feet across. It looked to be about ten to twenty feet deep. I recall seeing a little bright light about the size of a nickel or quarter in the center of the bottom of the well. At the time, I had a feeling as though a giant bear had me by the back and would not let go. This was very uncomfortable, and I felt as though I was in prison. I was angry about it. So I started talking to God about what I was feeling. I told Him I thought it was a dirty rotten deal for Him to give me this feeling of imprisonment just after allowing me to be run over by a drunk. My flying career was no doubt over. My family had almost lost a husband and father. I probably would never walk again, and now I was made to feel as though a giant bear clutched me in its claws or jaws.

A voice spoke back to me out of the little light. It told me that I had a problem with my relationship with God and that was the cause of the ugly feeling in my back. The voice said I did not realize I was just a creature of God, and He was first and always must be. I must remember that He made me and I was His son. In short, I needed to develop a spirit of submission, obedience, and humility if I expected my life to improve. The voice told me to put God first in my life and the feeling of entrapment would go away. I asked the Person in the light if I would never be able to fly again. The reply was, "I have not decided that yet." Then He said, "If you leave everything to me, you will be happier than you have ever been." I was told I would never have to worry about anything and whatever I needed would be provided. The implication was that I would be provided for financially, but if I ever wanted a job or needed one, with prayer it would be forthcoming. I had always worried a lot about everything. Now I was made to realize I need not worry. All my needs and my family's needs would be taken care of. At one point, the voice even said, "I am God and you are Ted. As soon as you get that straight, things are going to really brighten up for you."

So I gave in. I told God I knew I was only a creature, and He was the Creator and that everything we have comes from Him. Almost immediately, the pain and trapped feeling I had in my back totally left. I was aware of a tremendous peace. I have pretty much had that peace ever since. Our family has been well provided for, even though we have put six children through college and other training with no one in the family working.

I back slide at times. I am very human, and it is difficult to keep the right attitude. It was much easier just after the injury. I had a very close brush with death and that thought was in my mind just about all the time. But as time passes, it is easy to become lax and feel as though I had a right to all the blessings all along. I know that is not true. I know that my family and I have been truly blessed. God made a tremendous a promise to me and it has been more than fulfilled.

KATHERINE ANNE (KATIE) HERNANDEZ

From her earliest memory, little Katie Hernandez knew suffering, she was a victim soul. She lived just a few months beyond her fourth birthday, yet her life touched many of us in a powerful way.

I am deeply indebted to the entire Hernandez family. They allowed me to be an integral member of their special family. I have included two talks that I gave on the occasion of Katie's death; one on the night before her funeral, the other during the funeral Mass. I believe these talks capture the essence of a little girl that wound herself around our hearts and taught our community the meaning of suffering.

Katie is still exercising a powerful influence on our community. It was her death that pushed me into creating a prayer garden dedicated to Our Blessed Mother. It is done in honor of all of the infants and small children who died from our parish in the last twenty-seven years of our existence. May Katie touch your heart, as she did mine. Here is her story told in these talks

Mass - Friday, February 21, 1992
Our Special Angel

My brothers and sisters, tonight is not exactly

going to be a homily, but what I'd like to share with you from my heart is what this child has been for me, and I'm sure what Katie has been for many of you. Because I think that when a whole community prays as hard as we did for Katie to get well and she died, then there's always the danger that we will ask why is it that God didn't answer our prayers. I think that He did, that what the Father did for us was provide a special angel to care for and nurture us. What we remember of her is that she was and will be our special angel.

Unfortunately, because so many in the community never get the opportunity as I do, or as every priest does to be part of the very specialness of individual's lives, I'd like to share a few thoughts with you about Katie.

One of the most moving events for me in the last two months was when I went over to pray over Katie with Lou, Toni and the children. I'll never forget that moment because Katie was sitting on my lap and all of us had our hands on her head. Of course, as only I would do, I was praying that she get well. What we need to understand is how the Lord uses each one of us to minister to the other. When it came to her mother's turn, Toni prayed for her to get well but she also said, "But we pray for whatever God wills". It was almost as if finally after all these years, our Blessed Mother was able to get through my tough skull and say when we pray, we always pray the prayer of surrender. Not what we want but what God wants. And so what I would say to you, the first lesson I learned from this child was that prayer must begin and end in surrender.

I would never have believed that I would witness in my own lifetime, a four year old child making her First Communion.(2) But many people had come to me and said, "this child is ready, she knows the Eucharist is Jesus and First Communion". What a glorious event it was to see this little one not only receive Holy Communion but also the Sacrament of Confirmation. I remember that moment because her Confirmation went very well. But I was concerned about her reception of Holy Communion. After all, she was only a baby.

When it came time for her communion, I took the consecrated host and dipped it into the consecrated chalice, and I said to her mother that I would hand it to her and she would give it to Katie. But when her mother came up, she said, "No, she wants you to give her communion". Katie received that Eucharist with greater devotion than you will see in most Catholic Churches. This four year old child knew that communion was Jesus, and so we learn another lesson, the lesson of the importance of the Eucharist in the life of each one of us.

Another lesson that Our Blessed Mother taught me was a rather painful lesson that has taken a very long time to understand and that is, I never thought about Mary suffering under the cross. Of course, I had learned in Theology that one of the seven sufferings of Mary was seeing her Son suffer. But again, as I watched this mother holding her baby in great pain, the far greater pain was that of the mother.

It was as if a veil was lifted, and I could stand under the cross and see Mary and realize the enormity of her pain. Our Blessed Mother didn't just suffer seeing her child dying. She also suffered realizing that she was being bombarded by those angry, violent unbelievers and yet, she stood quietly and courageously and suffered.

Particularly for you young people, if anyone ever tells you that "sin doesn't hurt" or "everyone's doing it", you'd only have to stand under the cross for 30 seconds to realize that sin hurts, not only Jesus but His mother.

Katie was an angel for me because she allowed me entrance into her very special family, and that began really with the other children Tina, Leslie, Josh, and Patrick. There were moments when my heart seemed to be torn apart, and one of them would come up and hug me, and I knew that I belonged to that family, as I belong to each of your families.

A couple of nights ago when we were all expecting Katie to die, Patrick the youngest child in the Hernandez family didn't want to go to bed. His dad tried to put him to bed without success. First, he said he wanted his dad to hold him. That worked for about three or four minutes and then he decided he wanted me to hold him. I realized how very special this entire family is. I've already talked about Toni. Lou is the loving father, the strong support, the dad who will always be there for his children.

When it seemed as if Katie was about to die, the children came in and said, "Can we say the rosary?" After a few minutes, the mother stopped the child who was saying the Hail Mary, and said, "Are you praying with your heart?" How many times have we heard that, and it never really made any sense. But it's almost as if a mother can look into the heart of a child and say, "When you pray, don't just say the words. Let it flow from your heart."

It's obvious that Lou and Toni are products from their own wonderful parents. Lou comes from a family of ten children. What it must have been like to come from Cuba in the early 60's, to have the family separated and yet what has held them together has been the love for each other, and the love of their parents. You can see the effect that Toni's family has had on her, coming from a family of six. It is sad when young people tell me when they get married, "Well, we want a boy for him, and girl for her, and two children are all we ever want because we have to have all of the other things that are going to make us happy." If you want to know what this family has taught you, it's that our children are our treasures.

The gift that I also learned has been the enormity of love of this community. You've seen a little bit of that tonight -- how many people have reached out to this family.

The last thing I would say to you is that Katie really had the life of a victim soul. For most of her four years she has suffered. And suffering is very hard to understand. St. Paul tells us that we must suffer to make up what's lacking in the sufferings of Jesus Christ. That's a simple way of telling us that there's a redemptive quality in our suffering. In God's plan, He allows us to suffer and we don't really know why, but we know it's part of His plan.

She was chosen for a very special role, a victim soul. I believe it's because not just that she's a saint after only four years, but that she's going to have great impact in this community.

One of our college girls asked Katie, "Are you still my little angel?" She answered without hesitation, "Angela, I'll always be your angel." I believe that she'll be the guardian angel not only for that one person but for all of us.

I'd like to close with a poem that was written this week by Bernie Warren. A couple of nights ago, she had a dream and in this dream she saw this beautiful child lying on a beautiful altar surrounded by angels. She said there was a silver-blue aura around her. She woke up and she wrote this poem and I'd like to close with it. I would title her poem OUR SPECIAL ANGEL. It goes like this:

>Dearest Mommy and Daddy, sweet family and friends
>I want you all to know
>I got my wings today
>And how I love them so.
>
>Jesus gave me gold ones
>Because I'm special you see
>He loves me so very much
>That He saved them just for me.
>
>I'm a special angel
>And my job is special too
>I sit with my precious Jesus
>Which He gives to a special few.
>
>He said He'll keep me near Him
>To keep the incense close by
>You know your prayers will come up near me
>So pray everyone, I'll tell you why.
>
>Your prayers come up as incense
>And surround us all the time
>It's so very beautiful,
>I guess you would say sublime.
>
>Mommy and Daddy, you did the best you could
>So, please know that I love you
>Sisters and brothers, too.
>
>Father Carroll
>you're my very bestest friend
>I want you to know

I loved you until the very end.

Pray and I'll make very special effort
To get your prayers first in line
So if you smell roses
You'll know that this is the sign.

All my special young friends
Remember my vow to you
I'm your special angel

I really loved you too.
I must be about my job, now
And sit with my Jesus you see
So when you think of angels
Remember to think of me.
Love Katie.

Postscript

A few months after Katie's death, Lynn Glover, a parishioners, was dying. A short time before she died, Lynn shared this story with me. She saw Katie by her bedside. She told me how comforting it was to her in her final hours. Katie truly is Our Special Angel.

The next day Katie's funeral was held in St. Margaret Mary Church. I really don't know how I kept from crying, and yet this Mass was a celebration, knowing in our hearts that Katie was in Heaven. The talk below was given on this special day of Katie's burial.

Katherine Anne (Katie) Hernandez
Funeral Mass - February 22, 1992

My Dear Friends,

Last night, the word that we picked for Katie

was an "angel," she is our special angel. The word that I've selected this morning is "cross." The cross is the only thing that will explain to us the meaning of Katie's life, because we cannot have a resurrection without a crucifixion.

When I was on my sabbatical, I had begun to journal. I was very concerned because obviously, we were moving into a very trying time for the Church and the world. I began to write that *love* was the answer. I was awakened early one morning with a very little sign which made it very clear to me that it's the cross; that's the answer. It's the cross that will explain to us the meaning of Katie as the victim soul, because Katie lived for four years on that cross.

We need to remember the story that Jesus used in Numbers 21:4-9 of the Old Testament. The Jews had begun to sin when Moses went up the mountain and God afflicted His people. They were being bitten by snakes. When Moses returned and was asked to pray to God, he was told to make a bronze serpent. Whoever looked on the serpent was saved. Jesus used that very example and said, "Just as Moses lifted up the serpent in the desert, so must the Son of Man be lifted up, that all who believe may have eternal life in Him." (The Gospel of John 3:14-15) It's the cross that explains the meaning of our lives.

In today's Gospel, we read of the crucifixion. In your mind's eye, I would ask you to go back to that moment in history, to listen to what Jesus tells us from the cross. You heard Him crying out in pain, "My God, my God, why have you forsaken me?" When we first heard that cry, it sounds very much like the cry of our own prayers, a cry almost of despair - "Why God don't you listen?" But that was clearly a very minor meaning of what Jesus was saying. What Christ was praying was Psalm 22. It was a Messianic promise being fulfilled. Let me read to you just a few verses of Psalm 22. Just as we know the "Our Father" by heart, all of the Jews knew Psalm 22. And these were some of the things that He was fulfilling from Psalm 22:

"My God, my God, why have you forsaken me, far from my prayer, from the words of my cry? But I am a worm, not a man; the scorn of men, despised by the people. All who see me scoff at me; they mock me with parted lips, they wag their heads: I am like water poured out; all my bones are racked. My heart has become like wax melting away within my bosom. My throat is dried up like baked clay, my tongue cleaves to my jaws; to the dust of death you have brought me down. Indeed, many dogs surround me, a pack of evildoers closes in upon me; They have pierced my hands and my feet; I can count all my bones. They look on and gloat over me; they divide my garments among them, and for my vesture they cast lots."

What Jesus was crying from the cross was not a cry of despair. It was a reminder that the cross is the thing that saves us. Jesus is telling us that the cross is the plan of God the Father for our salvation.

Then we heard Jesus talking to His mother and to John the Apostle, in the Gospel of John 19:26-27, "... 'Woman, there is your son.' In turn he said to the disciple, 'There is you mother.'" By Jewish law, if Jesus had had blood brothers, He could not have committed His mother to someone who was not a relative. John was not a relative. In committing His mother to John, He was committing her to each one of us.

Mary was the only person who could have

stopped the pain I thought about as I saw Katie dying. If her mother had the power to stop the pain, she would have done so. Mary had the power to stop the crucifixion. You remember that in John's Gospel, he tells us about going into the outer courtyard. John obviously had some influence. While women could not testify in a trial, every mother had the right of appeal. John could have gotten Mary into the trial of the Sanhedrin. Mary could have said, "Stop it, my Son doesn't know what He wants." Mary could have stopped the crucifixion but she didn't. And so on the cross, she became our Mother.

You could see how Our Lady was Katie's mother. Last summer, when a Jehovah's Witness came to their home and was berating Toni, two year old Patrick went to Katie's room, stood on her bed and brought down a statue of Our Lady. He took the statue of Mary and put it in the living room, right in front of the Jehovah's Witness. Meanwhile, Katie got the book, *True Devotion to Mary*, from the bookshelf and brought it to the living room. It blew their minds. The Jehovah's Witness ran away.

"Father, into Your hands I commend my spirit." These final words that Jesus uttered were the prayer that Jesus learned from His mother, Mary. Every night, as a child the age of these children before me, Mary would say that prayer with Jesus. "Father, into Your hands I commend my spirit." (The Gospel of Luke 24:46) If Katie has a message to all mothers, it would be to teach your children to pray. Katie loved to pray, she loved to say the rosary. You have to see a four year old saying the rosary to know that only mothers can teach children to pray. You don't learn how to pray in Catholic schools. You learn to pray from your mother and Katie taught us this.

The cross was also a sign of unconditional love. When Jesus cried out, "I am thirsty." (The Gospel of John 19:28) He wasn't thirsting just for water; He was thirsting for our love. Christ said before He died, "there is no greater love than this: to lay down one's life for one's friends." (The Gospel of John 15:13) If there is something that Katie would teach us, it is that the cross is the path to love. All of the things that Mary has said in Medjugorje and throughout the world: prayer, fasting, the love of the rosary, going to church and loving the Mass, all relate directly to the cross. It reminds us in a very clear way that Jesus is all about love, that the cross will bring us to paradise. It's the way.

My memory of Katie will always be one of love. Like all the children in this family, you will never find more loving children. From the oldest to the youngeSt. I guess the memory I will cherish as long as I live happened just a couple of days before she died, when I was at my worst point Toni said to Katie, "Would you give Father a kiss?" Though she was in great pain, she gave me the most wonderful hug that I will never forget. The cross is all about love.

Finally, the cross was a cry of victory. This ceremony this morning is all about victory. "There was a great shout." Both *Matthew* (27:50) and *Luke*(23:46) tell of it. John does not mention the shout but he tells us that Jesus died having said, 'It is finished." (John 19:30). In the original that would be one word; and *that one word was the great shout.* 'Finished!' Jesus died with the cry of triumph on his lips, his task accomplished, his work completed, his victory won."(3) This morning is a cry of victory for Katie. She's carried that cross for four years. It's a cry of victory not of sorrow, knowing that the cross leads us to heaven. Nevertheless, the loss of someone so precious is always a deep hurt for all of us. In my own name, as well as the priests, deacons and all of the community, I'd like to express to Luis, Toni, the children, all the grandparents, members of the family and friends, our deep sympathy and assurance of our continued prayers for you. The real loss though is not in this child dying. The real loss would be if we come away without understanding the meaning of this child's life. It was all about life, all about love. The cross is the path to heaven. And this child pointed the way for you.

I would close with this poem that was given to me by someone I don't know - E.J.D.T.D. and it goes like this:

In Memory Of Katie

Do not grieve, my children
Your little one is now with me
She laughs and sings so sweetly
As she sits upon my knee.
I know that you'll miss her
But you see, I missed her too
She was a special little treasure
I only loaned to you.

Remember, my dear children,
this world is not your home
I prepared a place for you
very near my Father's throne.

And one day, very soon now
All my children will be here
I'll meet them as they enter
And I will wipe away their tears.

For that day, dear children
is what you've all been waiting for
We will feast at heaven's banquet
On that great celestial shore.

Katie was such an inspiration to all of us that I wanted some way for our children to be reminded of the young saints we have in heaven. The prayer garden, which lists the names of all our infants and young children that have died from St. Margaret Mary, is one way of looking for support when things aren't going well. I also put Katie's picture in Mary's window, over the entrance of the chapel. When we need help, Katie will be there, I am sure.

Recently, Imelda Besh told me this story. Her mother was dying and because of her own illness she couldn't visit her. Imelda knew her mother would be frightened, so she prayed to Katie. "Katie, please be with my mother," she pleaded. The next day, Imelda called her sister to inquire about their mother. "Mom keeps talking about a little girl with dark hair and dark eyes, who is in the room with her," the sister reported. "Mom says she is about four years old."

Nobody in St. Margaret Mary doubts that was Katie Hernandez, our special angel.

[1]R. Vincent, *Please Come Back To Me And My Son: Our Lady's Appeal Through Christina Gallagher* (Westmeath, N. Ireland: Ireland's Eye Publications, 1992), 41-42.

[2]Editors note: A priest friend sent word to remind me that Pope Pius X had given Holy Communion to a dying four year old almost a century ago.

[3]William Barclay, *The Gospel of Mark*, revised ed., (Pennsylvania: The Westminster Press, 1956), 364.

Chapter 4
PRAYERFUL CHILDREN

"...But Jesus said, 'Let the children come to me. Do not hinder them. The kingdom of God belongs to such as these.'"
The Gospel of Matthew 19:14.

In Sacred Scripture we learn that St. Paul gives instructions to a community that is applicable today. Paul, looking at this small band of believers and knowing the persecutions they would face, gives us one definition of a Remnant Church. A Remnant in its first meaning is defined as "a small surviving group". Certainly, Jesus meant this when He said, "When the Son of Man returns will He find any faith whatsoever?" The clear inference is that many would fall away from the faith.

The other definition given by Webster's Dictionary for remnant is "an unsold or unused end piece goods". Putting this in understandable terminology, I believe that the remnant community is both those who remain, i.e. have kept the faith, and also those who are unsold. That is those who have not sold out or been sold out by their shepherds to the values of the world, but remain firm to the values of Jesus Christ. They are the tatters of the garment of Jesus Christ, His Church. The Gospel tells us that love of one another is the sign that a community has not sold out to the world. Love is the sign of the tattered garment of Jesus Christ, His Church.

The percentage of Catholics in the world that take the message of Our Blessed Mother seriously is small. How many Catholics do you know that believe Mary's words that there will be a period of great trials, as described in Sacred Scripture; not the end of the world but trials that are truly devastating? I would submit to you the number of Catholics who live her messages of prayer and fasting is incredibly small. How many believe Josyp Terelya when he tells us that the time predicted in the Book of Revelation is now upon us? Those who listen will be part of the Remnant Church.

Listen with your hearts to St. Paul's advice and discover for yourself what Our Blessed Mother has been telling us for eleven years in Medjugorje. "We must undergo many trials if we are to enter into the Reign of God." "In each church", the Acts of the Apostles 15:23 says, "they installed presbyters (i.e. Priests) and, with prayer and fasting, commended them to the Lord in whom they had put their faith".

Everything St. Margaret Mary parish has done in the last few years has focused on building a sound spiritual foundation that will endure the coming trials; Eucharistic Adoration, devotion to the Immaculate Heart of Mary, the Cenacle on Wednesday nights, Prayer Groups and Peer Ministry, focus on the Holy Spirit. There is a tendency now as pastor to sit back and say, "Well, at least my children are prepared for any eventuality." And believe me at my age that is a real temptation.

But I feel that we are being drawn into the battle in a much more dramatic way. I feel the Holy Spirit wants us to become a Remnant Community, a parish that maintains our faith in Jesus Christ during the coming trials. I feel we are also being called to be a **REMNANT**, that is a sign to the world that we have not sold out to the values of the world.

I believe the Holy Spirit is calling us to that mission. How we accomplish this mission is where many will disagree. It is this vision of St. Margaret Mary that will take the prayerful discernment of many of us. It is very easy for pride to come in. When Our Blessed Mother constantly wants you to pray for priests, you should take Our Lady seriously!

Recently, we installed a window in the chapel entrance. The inspiration for that window comes from Revelation 12:1: "**A great sign appeared in the sky, a woman clothed with the sun, with the moon under her feet, and on her head a crown of twelve stars.**" This window reminds us of the **TRIUMPH OF THE IMMACULATE HEART OF Mary**. The entrance window which depicts a cross and the Eucharist reminds us of two important qualities of the Remnant Church; it must be Eucharistic and it must be Sacrificial. The Chapel window reminds us of the battle that will be waged. We will live to see the Triumph of the Immaculate Heart of Mary.

I spent considerable time with Howard Jenkins, the Superintendent of Education. I shared briefly what Bobby Ohler, our Principal, four teachers and I learned about computerization of schools from a recent visit to Shawnee Mission Public School in Kansas. By the end of next year, our school will be one of the finest in the country.

I told Mr. Jenkins that I would like St. Margaret Mary to be used as a model school for the Archdiocese. We would be willing to train other teachers for a total computerized school. In return, I asked that our school staff be allowed to make a presentation at the National Catholic Education Conference (N.C.E.A.) in April, 1993, which will be in New Orleans. Mr. Jenkins agreed and this has been worked out. We will speak at the N.C.E.A.

convention in April.

Why am I anxious to showcase our school? Why the focus on computers?

What others will see when they visit this school in the fall of 1993 is the real vision. Mr. Ohler, has lengthened the religion class from 30 to 50 minutes a day. One period a week is a prayer experience. We hired a young man, Mike Clavijo, as our youth minister and 40 volunteer mothers teach our children to pray. The Cenacle of prayer consists of recitation of the rosary, singing with Clavijo and other forms of prayer.

What connection do I see between the computers and being a Remnant Church? In themselves, there is no connection. However, if our school becomes a true ministry where prayer is integral, the fabulous network of computers will be an entree. It will expose other schools to the POSSIBILITY OF PRAYER.

Certainly, we could hide our light! But I think the Holy Spirit is calling us to become not just a remnant, a small group that holds on to the faith, but the tattered garment of Jesus that shows the world what real love is. Our society has robbed many children in this country of hope because they refuse to allow values to be taught in public schools. The mayor of Washington recently announced her solution to the AIDS epidemic by giving every public high school and middle school child free condoms and free needles to drug addicts.

St. Margaret Mary may one day be a model school not because of computers or other technology but because of the ability of our children to pray. The weekly prayer meeting will empower these children to excel in prayer.

Now you know the rest of the story. Our community was called to build a model school but what makes it truly unique is not the technology, but the fact that our children are discovering the powerful tool of prayer, particularly the rosary.

In a presentation to the National Catholic Education Conference in April, 1993, I will have the opportunity to issue an invitation. Our principal, Bobby Ohler, and our computer specialists, Leo Craiglow and Jane Reynolds, will extol the advantages of computers and other technology in a parochial school. As the pastor of our "MODEL SCHOOL," I will invite every pastor and principal involved in the parochial school system to join us in BUILDING A NET OF PRAYER utilizing our parochial school children.

My message to them will be this…**"Save the Church. Teach our children to pray, particularly the Rosary. Do this and you will be A REMNANT CHURCH."**

Chapter 5
THE ARK

"Then God's temple in heaven opened and in the temple could be seen the Ark of the Covenant. There were flashes of lightning and peals of thunder, an earthquake, and a violent hailstorm."
Revelation 11:19.

"A Great sign appeared in the sky, a woman clothed with the sun, with the moon under her feet, and on her head a crown of twelve stars."
Revelation 12:1.

"Pray, Pray, Pray!"
Message of Our Lady at Medjugorje

It was Saturday night, July 18, 1992, when I saw CNN News. It showed hundreds of children, many of them homeless, being moved by bus from war-torn Sarajevo. These children were being moved to a safe location first to Split in Yugoslavia, then on to Italy. I am sure many of them wondered if they would ever return. I was reminded what Marija Pavich, a visionary from Yugoslavia, had said a few months earlier when she visited in Baton Rouge, Louisiana She told us that what is happening in Yugoslavia may well happen here. "Every country would experience the coming trials, learn from Yugoslavia!" she said.

Suddenly, all the recent memories of warning converged upon me. We had heard Josyp Terelya tell us that the time predicted in the Book of Revelation was upon us. Fr. Tim Deeter, pastor in Orangefield, Texas, gave a talk at St. Margaret Mary Church. He was told by Our Lady that his parishioners should pray for priests. There will be a schism in the United States. Prepare for persecution!

My great fear is that part of the trial for us will be schism, or apostasy. "The unity both of Faith and of communion is guaranteed by the Primacy of the Pope, the Supreme teacher and Pastor of the Church .... One is cut off from the unity of faith by heresy and from the unity of communion by Schism."(1) This is caused by a denial of an essential Catholic belief..moral or dogma. Fr. Jozo, a holy priest from Medjugorje who visited the United States said: "The schism has already begun."

The Saturday morning paper may have been one of the first warnings. It reported the Catholic Church's position on homosexuality. The Vatican had confirmed that "homosexuality is an objective disorder. Governments should deny privileges to gays to promote traditional family values and protect society." The example they gave was the consignment of children for adoption and foster care and the employment of teachers or coaches. Sadly, the paper reported the reaction of a priest who works with gays, "I don't think any American would put serious stock in this statement." It was as if this priest hadn't heard of the Catholic Church's longstanding position on homosexuality.

I believe the full blown schism will begin soon after the publication of the universal catechism recently approved by Pope John Paul II. It will be published in the United States by Easter of 1993. The French translation has already been published. The Holy Father seemed to expect this when he wrote, "the new catechism will put an end to teaching or interpretations of the faith, or morals, which are not in accord with each other or the magisterium."

THE REMNANT CHURCH
Components Of The Ark

I believe we are being called to build a community that is totally loyal to the Pope and the teachings of the Catholic Church. If the prophesies come true, many will break from the church. The remnant will be those who remain faithful to the teachings of Jesus in the coming trial. Jesus said, "when the Son of Man comes, will He find any faith whatsoever?"

We have covered three characteristics of a Remnant Church. We have worked to develop a strategy to prepare our parish to face the trials predicted by Our Lady. These characteristics are:

1. A Eucharistic Community - one that believes Jesus is truly present in the Holy Eucharist.
2. A Marian Community - one that has great devotion to Mary, the Mother of Jesus.
3. A Suffering Community - one that bears the pain of loss of infants and children and nourishes the elderly.

I believe another piece of the puzzle for our community at St. Margaret Mary is our parochial school. For it will be through the school that our children will learn to pray. Because of the technological advances being made, this school will be a model parochial school for our entire area.

Just over a year ago, we had a parents meeting to discuss declining enrollment at St. Margaret Mary School. In two years, we had lost 100 students. The parents expressed the need for us to prepare for the next century. "Build a computer lab," they said, "and we will pay for it."

In the summer of 1991, we completed a large

computer lab with a total of 43 computers networked together. Later in the school year, we began the computerization of the library and administration area. Registration took a dramatic turn upward. Yet I felt driven in light of the dire predictions about coming trials. Why was I so concerned about the parochial school? "Perhaps we need to think about a retreat center in a secluded area," some suggested. I didn't know why, but somehow I sensed that the parochial school is a part of God's plan for this community.

Two events conspired to convince me that we cannot bury our gifts. After visiting Shawnee Mission School District with our principal, Bobby Ohler, and four teachers, we became convinced that the future of parochial schools lies in technology.

About the same time, Archbishop Schulte discussed with the deans a planned 20 million dollar drive for Catholic education. I realized at that meeting that the Lord wants us to help save the inner city parochial schools. In order to do that together, we must build a 21st century school, utilizing modern technology. We must provide a model.

I made an offer to the Superintendent of Education that we would be willing to become a model school. I suggested that the Archdiocese should spend money to support technology for the inner city schools. We have been told by priests in the area that if the planned subsidy goes to teacher salaries only, these inner city schools will be forced to close.

Because of the efforts of the superintendent, four of us, the pastor, principal and two teachers were invited to participate in a conference at the

University of Dayton entitled, "Frontiers in Catholic Education." Eleven parochial schools throughout the United States and Canada were asked to participate. Ten of our school staff had already gone to Dallas for a software convention, and we had just purchased an additional 80 computers for the classroom. We were well prepared for this event that occurred during the summer of 1992.

The Dayton conference was a success, as the eleven schools selected were to draw up a plan for parochial schools for the 21st century. The speakers reinforced our conviction that we were on the right road, but much more must be done.

One of the speakers, Bob Tinker spoke Saturday night. "Computers are only tools," he said. "Much more is necessary for a 21st century school." I didn't understand what he was driving at until I awoke at 4:00 a.m. the next morning. It was crystal clear. Build an ark!

All of a sudden it all came together. God was displeased with His people. He told Noah to build an ark before He punished them. He gave him the tools. The plan seemed incomplete, 300 x 50 cubits long, by 30 cubits wide. We would have wanted detailed plans and specifications. Then the flood came.

Perhaps God is giving us a chance to build a new ark. The purpose of this ark is much the same as the dream of the early American Bishops when they mandated a Catholic school in every parish at a council in Baltimore. Their purpose was twofold; save the faith of our children; and secondly, they knew that the children would bring their parents to Jesus.

For many years it worked. Until 1960, 85% of

our Catholic people used to go to church every Sunday. The nuns made sure that if your parents didn't go, you would pray them back into the church. Something is already happening to our parochial school that will bring back the same sense of the presence of Christ that the nuns gave to us prior to Vatican II.

Because we have begun to try to live the messages of Our Lady at Medjugorje and because we have spent an hour a week in adoration of the Blessed Sacrament, this entire place has become Holy Ground. But we must finish the task.

THE APOSTOLATE OF HOLY MOTHERHOOD

I spoke at all the Masses on the weekend of July 25th and 26th, 1992, on the *Apostolate of Holy Motherhood*. I gave out free books to the mothers and grandmothers who were willing to join in this prayer crusade. Forty mothers volunteered to help conduct a fifty minute Cenacle of prayer during one of the children's five religion periods.

The Apostles asked Jesus, "Lord, teach us to pray." This is the same prayer that we make today, for prayer is our urgent need. I believe the Holy Spirit is issuing a special call to all mothers to embark on a spiritual journey. I am here to enlist you in an army of prayer.

We have heard for some months that this is the year of the woman. For politicians, this means that more women will be elected to Congress. For others, this is a subliminal message. if you want to get elected, you must support abortion rights for women. You are being told by these purveyors of death to the unborn that, "women have the right to choose." One and a half million women a year choose to kill their children.

Sin is epidemic! Less than half of Catholic marriages survive. A million children a year are added to the numbers already growing up in our country with one parent. The hurt that these innocents experience because of divorce is unfathomable. The average length of a marriage today is five years. One in five white children and two out of every three black children are born into a home without a father. Sexual abuse abounds.

Those who have become victims of Satan's fury, parents and children have our deep concern and the daily prayers of our community.

Most of us lack the ability or the courage to fight against the onslaught of abortion in the world. Few of us know what to do to ward off the attacks by the evil one against Christian marriages. We feel helpless.

The Holy Spirit has given the church a partial remedy. That remedy is the *Apostolate of Holy Motherhood*. I believe it is a call from God to rally the church to the side of our dear children who are besieged today.

It is no secret in this community that those who pray best are the mothers of our parish. These women know better than any man ever will, the meaning of surrender. And surrender is the key element in meaningful prayer.

Every married woman caught up in the ecstasy of love uttered her first surrender when she agreed to marry her spouse. She repeated that act of surrender publicly on her wedding day when she said, "I do." And every child she has given birth to is a repetition of Our Blessed Mother's beautiful words, "Fiat, I will it; let it be done according to thy will!"

I asked mothers who are members of the Apostolate of Holy Motherhood to volunteer one hour a week to help lead these Prayer Meetings or Bible Readings for the younger children. "If you feel that the Holy Spirit is leading you to this ministry, I would ask that you sign up."

It is significant that one of the major reasons young people leave the Catholic Church is that they were never taught to pray. The experts at prayer in this community are our mothers.

I believe that within two years, a large number of educators will be coming to the town of Slidell to learn about the parochial school in the 21st century. The greatest gift we can give them is to show them children who have learned to pray and have a great love of Jesus and His Mother Mary. And this will happen because of women who belong to the Apostolate of Holy Motherhood.

The Apostles asked Jesus, "Lord teach us to pray." The Holy Spirit is asking all mothers both at home and in our school, "teach our children to pray."

Jesus showed us the importance of surrender to prayer. When asked by His disciples, "Lord teach us to pray." Jesus said, "Say, Our Father who art in heaven, Thy will be done on earth as it is done in heaven." Thus surrender is essential to prayer.

The best hope married men have of Heaven is to learn surrender from their spouse. A year ago, I gave a talk on marriage and talked about surrender. A few days later a married woman came in to tell me a beautiful story. She and her husband had decided to get a divorce. This would have been their final Mass together. When I spoke of surrender, they looked at the crucifix behind me.

In the entire church, they were the only two who saw a special light shining on the cross. It was their sign. "Surrender!" "We are not getting a divorce," the woman concluded, "we are going to work it out."

Jesus said in the Gospel of John 15:13, "There is no greater love than this: to lay down one's life for one's friends." The gift of surrender was taught to all of us on the hard bed of Calvary. No one understands this lesson as well as a mother.

There are three basic tenets the members of the *Apostolate of Holy Motherhood* must follow:

1. They must devote all their time, energy and resources, including their very selves to the greater glory of God and the pursuit of the divine will in their lives.
2. They must be consecrated to the Divine Mother under the title of Mother of God.
3. They must fulfill their daily duties as mothers and wives in an exemplary manner of holiness by pursuing the contemplative life in their homes.

The Heart of the Movement and major points of the *Apostolate of Holy Motherhood* are:

1. An Apostolate of Mothers consecrated to the Mother of God, for the Glory of God.
2. Pursuit of divine will in their lives.
3. Contemplative prayer.
4. Eucharistic Adoration.
5. Practice of Evangelical purity (Faithful to your vows).
6. Devotion to the Christ Child.
7. Devotion to the Holy Family (communication of the faith to their children.)
8. Fifteen decade daily Rosary.

9. Wearing of the Scapular and the Sacred Heart Badge.
10. Intense sacramental life (frequent Confession and Communion.)
11. Devotion to the Sacred and Immaculate Hearts.
12. Practice of the Nine First Fridays and Five First Saturdays (reparation for sin.)
13. Devotion to duty.
14. Fidelity to the Holy Father, the Magisterium, and all the teachings of the Church (both faith and morals).
15. Upholding of all the moral teachings of the Church.
16. Prayers for purity in the world.(2)

What will surprise you most about this spiritual movement for mothers is that many of these things you are already doing. The purpose is to "Help stem the tide of evil raging in so many families."

Bobby Ohler, has agreed to lengthen the religion period from 30 minutes a day to 50 minutes. Once a week each class has a prayer meeting in Church with our youth minister, Mike Clavijo. The mothers help lead these prayer meetings and our children are learning to pray.

CONCLUSION

Building an ark is more than remodeling a parochial school for the 21st century. The secret of building this ark rests with each of us: Pastor, parishioners, principal, students and staff, parents, mothers, fathers, grandparents and children. We will all have a hand in building the ark, for it will encompass the C.C.D. students, as well as the parochial students. For this dream to work we must all become like little children. For the ark is not made of wood, it is made of dreams, and the dream we share is that of Heaven itself. This ark will protect the faith of our children. Many others will not be so fortunate during the coming times of trials. So we have called this ark .. the remnant.

I have a sense that most of the pieces of the plan for the ark are now coming together. Like Noah, we have at times agonized how the plan for the ark was to work. If we have listened carefully to the Holy Spirit and followed His instructions, we will soon know if it floats.

This book has as its focus the importance of being on the ark of Peter. It is the teaching of the Catholic Church that Christians in good faith will go to Heaven. We have no intention or desire to limit God's magnificent goodness. Nor do we want to see Heaven only peopled by 144,000 individuals. We would be presumptuous to think we are that good. But we do want to reach out to fallen away Catholics and those outside the Catholic Church and to encourage you to seek the true faith. If you do, you will be on board when the ark sets sail.

The ark is more than a refuge, it is place of hope. Even a small light shines brightly in darkness. Your light will bring many home to their Heavenly Father. You too, in your own parish can help build an ark ... Remnant Church.

As you know, in the Old Testament it speaks not only of the ark constructed by Noah, which was a place of refuge. It also tells of the ARK OF THE COVENANT. In Exodus, an ark was built to house the covenant between God and Man. It was a cedar chest where the presence of God resided.

The ark we build may well be the enclosure to

protect the faith of our people, particularly our children. For the times of great trial, according to St. Paul in 2 Thessalonians, will be the loss of the Catholic Faith. The Jews lost the ark of the Covenant. It is the prayers of children that will preserve the treasure, Our Catholic Faith. To be a Remnant Church, we must construct not only a place of hope to withstand the flood of evil, but a tabernacle where the **very presence of God resides in the Holy Eucharist.**

[1]Dr. Ludwig Ott, *Fundamentals of Catholic Dogma* (St. Louis, Missouri: B. Herder Book Company, 1954), p. 301.

[2]Mark Miravalle, *The Apostolate of Holy Motherhood* (Milford, OH. 45150: The Riehle Foundation, P.O. Box 7, 1991), p. xii; xi-xii.

Chapter 6
EVANGELIZATION

"Then He told them: 'Go into the whole world and proclaim the good news to all creation.'"
The Gospel of Mark 16:15.

Evangelization is another characteristic of the REMNANT COMMUNITY. One of the constant calls issued by our Holy Father, Pope John Paul II, has been for evangelization. The meaning of this word is to spread the good news of Jesus Christ.

Perhaps one of the most misunderstood statements of the Second Vatican Council comes from the decree on ecumenism. In the spirit of fraternity, the document stresses the positive...there is truth and goodness in every Christian church.

For Catholics, this is not a surprising statement. Even our worst critics will acknowledge that you will never hear a sermon in a Catholic church criticizing another religion, despite the fact that our church is often the butt of many slanderous sermons. We try to put into practice the teaching of Jesus: "By this will all men know you are my disciples, that you have love for one another."

However, this statement on ecumenism has led many in the Catholic Church to play down the importance of trying to win converts to the Church. For the remnant community, evangelization, trying to win converts to the Lord, will be a sign.

Since 1983, the change at St. Margaret Mary has been remarkable. In that year, we began the Right of Christian Initiation of Adults, (R.C.I.A.) program. Utilizing the faith experiences of other

Catholics as leaders, our convert classes have grown each year. We have averaged over 20 adult converts a year since the R.C.I.A. started.

PRACTICAL STEPS

There are a number of ways our community evangelizes. I have already written about the parochial school. Clearly the early American bishops saw the parochial school as a tool of evangelization. I am also convinced that the C.C.D. program is an effective tool for evangelization. Unfortunately, many of our children fall away from the faith because their parents don't even attend church.

The Confirmation catechumenate is an effective tool of evangelization. All students from the 8th through the 11th grades attend scripture sharing sessions six times in the fall and six times in the spring. We have outlined Barclay's scriptural exegesis for the entire New Testament. All of our youth are expected to read and pray over the entire New Testament prior to confirmation in their senior year. The seniors attend a Life In The Spirit retreat before confirmation and are asked to make Jesus the Lord of their lives prior to receiving the sacrament of Confirmation.

Evangelization Through Peer Ministry

Four years ago at the insistence of one of our high school seniors, we established a Peer Ministry group called "Embraced." Since this group began, they have conducted a number of retreats modeled after the Life In the Spirit seminars.

In the retreats, the youth share their own experience. We have had young people tell of attempted suicide or coping with drugs and sexual problems. They have told of their return to grace and the enormity of the love of Jesus Christ. The most effective speakers I have ever heard have come from this group of peer ministers. Many of the sermons priests give come from the head; these young people speak from the heart.

I have asked two of our peer ministers to share portions of their talk with you. Both Katherine Alpha and David Cry are college students. They are also converts. Their testimony is a powerful witness to the work of the Holy Spirit in this community.

Katherine Alpha

When I was first asked to give a talk on this retreat, I was very excited and also a little scared. I have so much to say, but the problem is "how to say it". I certainly do not want to preach to you because I am not anymore "holier" than anyone else. I just want to share my experiences with you.

I have been living in Slidell for seven years, and I have been a Catholic for four years. I grew up as a Protestant until the age of 15. Everything changed when my Mom and Uncle Kenneth decided to go to Medjugorje. They were going half way across the world to see a woman I barely knew. Her name was Mary. As a Protestant, I knew Mary was the mother of God, and that is all. I didn't know much about her until my mother returned from her trip. Mom and Uncle Kenneth were filled with excitement and a lot of questions.

After hearing all about the apparitions and Mary, I instantly believed! I didn't see why anyone would or could fake something so beautiful! After their return, we started visiting the Catholic Church. This was truly an experience! Mass was the strangest thing because everyone else knew what to say, when to say it, when to sit and when to stand. I used to sit there and try and figure out how everyone knew what to do. Eventually I got the hang of it and started enjoying Mass.

Religion became the main topic in the Alpha house. Everyone believed except one of my uncles, although this soon changed. On Thanksgiving night of 1987, we were all outside looking at the stars when the word "Medjugorje" arose. My Uncle Scott decided to test God and he said, "If the messages of Medjugorje and apparitions are true, I want to see a shooting star right there! " (He pointed to a particular spot in the sky). Uncle Kenneth, with blind faith, told us to join hands and pray the "Our Father," asking God to give us this sign.

My cousin and I thought that this was true entertainment because my family never prays! We all joined hands and I was looking at the spot my uncle pointed to. If something was going to happen, I was going to see it! We started praying the "Our Father," and I was still laughing a little, until five or ten seconds into the prayer. A shooting star flew across the sky in the exact spot my uncle wanted. When I saw the star I screamed! I can still feel the drop of my heart every time I think of it. I had no doubt in my mind that God existed and that Mary and her messages were true! After this experience, my father, mother, brother, two uncles and I all became Catholics. Uncle Scott is not a Catholic, but now he does attend a Catholic Mass each week.

Now that we were Catholics, the journey had just begun. Mary was my patron saint when I was confirmed and she has always been so special to me. I always used to see pictures of her and statues and think, "I'll bet she is more beautiful than I can imagine! " One night, I had the chance to see her. I was sleeping on the floor in my room when I awoke to a huge blue light in my doorway. The light was in the shape of Mary with her hands out-stretched. The face would change from Mary to Jesus and back to Mary. At first, I thought I was dreaming until I realized that I was sitting up with my legs crossed and my chin on my hands. All I felt was complete peace. I did not receive any messages, all I felt was peace.

Now you may think that I am crazy, but I will now set up the past couple of years for you. I went to Northshore High School for four years. I was on the dance team "Silverbells" for three years, "Class Favorite" for all four years, "Homecoming Queen" and "Miss Northshore". To the world, I was living every high school girl's dream, but I had a shell of external happiness and an inside of turmoil. Mary and Jesus were last on my list of priorities. It was not until I started praying the rosary and trying to become closer to God that I started being happy. I've found that "Spirituality" is a constant struggle. I usually take one step forward and eight steps back. I have always done things the "Katherine Alpha" way. Then after I mess up, I go to God and ask for His help. One thing I have learned is to be humble. No matter how talented, good looking, smart or whatever you are, there is always someone better than you and someone better than them. I have learned to treat people equally and look inside the person not only at their shell.

If there is one thing that Mary is, she is "total beauty". She is radiant with love and kindness and her beauty shines through her, not at her. I know she wants to bring us closer to God and she has had a struggle with me. I want to be closer to God, but I want to do it my way and that is not possible.

I have to struggle everyday. I open the door a little but some days I slam it shut, but I always receive help. All you have to do is open the door to your heart one-half of an inch and let Mary take you to her Son.

David Cry

This talk is about why we need God in our lives, and the steps we must take to invite Jesus into our world. When I consider the valleys that I have walked through, I understand the need for God and have, because of the blessings that He has given me, invited Jesus into my life. At times my relationship with God has been an uphill battle. You see, it wasn't until recently that I realized exactly what God means to me.

My only hope today in sharing a part of my life with you is that we may all realize what God means to us.

Society, as we know it, has seen constant progression towards a preoccupation with materialism. At times, it seems as if the type of clothes that we wear and the cars that we drive are more important than the things that we think, or the emotions we feel. Although I see nothing wrong with dressing well or having a few nice things, when I was younger, I found myself consumed with materials and status. It was always important for me to feel like I fit in. The group of people I associated with were always the most popular and the activities we participated in, regardless of how juvenile they were, were always considered, "The thing to do." I wanted it all, regardless of the cost. The only thing that I didn't realize was that I didn't really have any understanding of what I wanted. God was of very little importance to me at that time of my life. I went to church on Sunday, but it wasn't because of what God had to offer. Rather, I wanted to be seen and considered a good person. I'd dress up and sit there and while I could be seen, my mind was usually a million miles away. The thing that I never seemed to realize was that there was a reason for me being there. Whether I knew it or not, God had a plan for my life. I was just too selfish to see it.

You see, during that period of my life nothing ever affected me. Realizing that I had done something wrong was almost impossible. I used to lie to my parents, teachers, and friends without even realizing what I had done. If what I said or did hurt someone, I didn't care. I convinced myself that I was the only person that mattered and if someone couldn't accept that, it was their problem, not mine. I'd do anything to keep running with the in crowd, even if it meant lying. I know that I hurt a lot of people because of the way I acted, but if you weren't like me I didn't care. What I couldn't see was that being with the right people didn't exactly turn out the way I had planned. The pressure that I felt, whether it was to keep drinking, stay out too late or sneak around doing childish things was immense. Often times, my "friends" added to my never ending confusion. All of the questions I had, remained unanswered and my insecurities continued to grow. Not only was I obnoxious but I was ignorant as well.

After I had ended my relationship, I received a call from a good friend who invited me to Mass. Although I wasn't Catholic, I agreed and soon found myself at St. Margaret Mary. Even though I wasn't able to fully participate in the Mass, I soon found an inner peace that was foreign to me. As these feelings grew, so did my curiosity. God knew that I needed guidance and direction as He answered my prayers by giving me a very beautiful person that I could rely on. One night, I reached out to that special friend and the doors that had been closed for so long began to open. As our conversation dragged on into the wee hours of the morning, she told me about Perpetual Adoration in the chapel at our church. Much to my surprise, I found myself on my knees before Jesus at 2:30 a.m., asking God for patience, understanding and perseverance. The weeks and months that followed amazed me as I enrolled in the R.C.I.A. classes and attended Mass on a daily basis.

This past Easter, I finally realized what God wanted for me as I was confirmed into the Church and received my first communion. Looking back, I think that the most amazing realization that I've come to is that I never made the decision to become Catholic. When God started to lead me to where He wanted me, I opened up to Him. Because of that oneness, I was blessed with the faith that has carried me to where I am now.

Today, we all have a choice. We can live the selfish and unconcerned life that I used to, or we can invite Jesus into our lives and experience what it means to feel His presence. Our decisions are important to the Lord, but He will not force His way into our lives. As it says in Jeremiah; "When you call to Me, and come to Me, I will listen to you. When you seek Me, you shall find Me." I'd like to see us all make an effort to seek Him. Knowing that my decisions have brought me the happiness, joy and peace that I had always considered unattainable, I feel confident that by inviting Him into our lives, we may all have better personal relationships and a genuine sense of what love is all about.

****

The music ministry and the adult leadership that accompanies these retreats have been awesome: Mark and Debbie Hargrave, John and Kathy Mire, Julia Spear, Mike Borgatti, Joey Parr, Deacon John Weber and his wife Jaynell, Theresa Calamari, Paul Rohlinger, Patricia Calamari, Sharlin Whitford, Lori Mire, Angela Besh, Mike Clavijo, Katherine Alpha, John and Jennifer Besh, David Cry, Amanda Hover, and a host of other volunteers who have served as discussion leaders at one retreat or another.

It is amazing to me how the Holy Spirit has used this group of peer ministers. In the summer of 1991, our group held a retreat at Gulf Shores, Alabama. A small group was on the beach during recreation when a harried mother rushed up to them. "Please help me," she screamed, "I have been searching for my small child. The last time I saw him, he was in the water."

Instead of panicking, they said to the mother, "Let's pray!" They joined hands and asked God's help. A few minutes later, as they scoured the beach, they found the little lost boy and returned him to his mother. The next day, the mother met some of the youth and told them her story. "I am a Protestant, single mother. I had given up on God, but your example has brought me back to Jesus Christ."

Evangelization Through Prayer

One of the chief benefits of Perpetual Adoration has been an increase in conversions to the Catholic Church. It is one thing to say that you believe in the Real Presence of Jesus Christ, a far different thing to practice that belief through adoration. The example of hundreds of men, women and children praying before the exposed monstrance in the chapel has brought many into the Church, as well as assisted in bringing back to the Church fallen away Catholics.

Welcome Home For Christmas

A few years ago, St. Margaret Mary borrowed an idea that had been tried in Florida. We distributed four issues of an evangelization newspaper encouraging those who had fallen away to "return home." The week before Christmas, we sent a personal invitation to every family. The invitation read... "Jesus Christ invites you to a meal", then listed the times of our Christmas Masses. We were flooded with children who returned to their Father's house that day.

THE POWER OF THE EUCHARIST

St. Paul tells us that: "the unbelieving spouse will be sanctified by the believer." We always encourage the Catholic partner to pray for the gift of faith for their spouse. But the most powerful prayers come from the children.

Prior to their first communion, I ask the children who will be making their first communion to pray for their parents who might be away from the Church. A couple came to the office to ask that their marriage be blessed in the Church. "Our daughter has prayed us back into Church," they told me.

St. PAUL'S GUILD

You, have heard it said frequently that converts make the best Catholics. This is certainly true. A number of converts started a group in our parish called The St. Paul's Guild. Once a month they have a guest speaker to talk about some aspect of the Catholic faith. They are a tremendous support group for new Christians, and adult education for "all" as to what Catholics believe.

Evangelization Drive

Few things cause as much stress to Catholic pastors as a diocesan fund drive. When Archbishop Schulte mandated a $20,000,000 drive, earmarking funds for the seminary, aged priests retirement, and school subsidy for the inner city schools, most pastors were frightened by the size of this goal.

We were then told that 40% of the funds generated by this drive would go to any parish program that was approved by the Archbishop. We were instructed to write our parish plan detailing how we would spend our portion of the funds raised.

It became quite clear to me that St. Margaret Mary would focus on EVANGELIZATION. We had just completed our third Evangelization newspaper entitled *"EVANGELIZATION 2000."* The funds that we raise will go toward an Evangelization building. In this structure, we will have an adult library, video library and space for our R.C.I.A. classes. Additional meeting rooms will be provided.

Most importantly, this drive will give us the opportunity to evangelize. The workers will be giving a copy of this book, *The Remnant Church*, to every family that they visit. The volunteers will stress a personal invitation to belong to this remnant parish. Far more important than raising funds will be the opportunity to invite back to the Church those who have left and to encourage the non-catholic spouses to consider belonging to St.

Margaret Mary.

Since the first printing of this book, we completed this evangelization program. Every Catholic family was visited and presented with a copy of this book. They were invited to belong to this Remnant Church. It was an occasion for healing many of the past hurts that they had received. On Wednesday of Holy Week we had mass and a healing service. After completing the primary purpose of their visit, evangelization, the workers mentioned that they could pledge for the Archdiocesan Endowment Campaign and Parish Evangelization Center. Incredibly, nearly a half million dollars was pledged.

CONVERSION

Every convert that enters the Catholic Church has a story to tell. I have asked Veralyn Alpha to share the story of her family with you. For the complete story, I would encourage you to read the book by Mrs. Alpha entitled *A Protestant Who Crossed the Bridge*. This is Veralyn Alpha's abridged story.

A Protestant Who Crossed The Bridge
VERALYN R. ALPHA

Although I have been a Protestant all of my life, attended church each Sunday and believed in God, I have never been an overly religious person. My life was normal and uneventful. However in October, 1987, my entire life changed. That is when my brother and I traveled to Medjugorje, Yugoslavia. I never dreamed that one day I would be a Catholic because to be perfectly honest, I always believed that Catholics thought they were better than everyone else. I am now proud to say that on March 25, 1989, not only did I become

Catholic, but my husband, two teenagers and two brothers also converted.

"Why did my brother and I go to Medjugorje?" We were both searching as our mother and grandmother were both diagnosed with cancer in October, 1985. Our father had a heart attack six months later and then a suspicious lump was removed from my breaSt. Our lives seemed to be falling apart. Our mother died in July, 1986, and the furious storm that had threatened us for eleven months seemed to be over.

When we entered the R.C.I.A. two years later, our class was asked, "Do you think you are here by choice or were you led here?" I now know that I was led into the Catholic Church by an unusual enormous 360 degree full circle rainbow around the sun. My husband and I witnessed this oddity on October 21, 1986, while driving along the Interstate. After curious calls to a TV station weather department, they could only guess it was "ice crystals." However, I circled the date on my calendar for I was sure that it meant something! It was forgotten for approximately two and a half years, but while updating my journal, a few dates seemed familiar. I raced up to the attic to retrieve the calendar I had saved along with my taxes. It confirmed that the date I returned home from Medjugorje, a "new" person was exactly one year later October 20, 1987. Another year later October 20, 1988, was the date of our first R.C.I.A. lesson, the night that our family took a firm step to change our faith! As the day began on each morning of October 21, '87 and '88, it was a new day a - new dawn! It was our covenant from God, just as it had been for Noah promising that the storm was over and a new spiritual life waited ahead for all of us!

I have since learned that this unusual

occurrence was indeed a "solar phenomenon." The Pittsburgh Center for Peace reported in their *Queen of Peace, Special Edition II* (Winter 1992-1993) that a rainbow around the sun was witnessed by millions at noon on June 9, 1991, as the missionary image of Our Lady of Guadalupe left Mexico city. A picture of the phenomenon accompanied the explanation. The paper reported, "It was in this manner that Our Lady first appeared to Juan Diego on Dec. 9, 1531. The sun appeared as a brilliant cloud, which in turn was surrounded by a round rainbow." To discover six and a half years later that it was perhaps the Mother of God who had appeared to us as Protestants was a wonderful feeling. Our lives completely changed exactly one year later.

For Protestants, Mary is only mentioned at the birth and death of Jesus. Therefore I felt there was a gap in my faith and I wanted to find out if everything I had heard about Medjugorje was true. I traveled there as a skeptical Protestant with my brother Kenneth, in October 1987. Upon our arrival, we were told that Mary is the mother of us all, not just Catholics. Although I witnessed the miracle of the sun and the cross spinning, I continued questioning everything and everyone. However, it was not the things that I did see that convinced me that everything was real. It was things that I "did not see" but could only feel. On a cold drizzly October night, on Apparition Hill, I was fortunate enough to be seated next to the visionaries. They began praying the Rosary and suddenly they stopped in mid-sentence, all at the same syllable. Their mouths were moving but no words came out! There was complete silence and all you could hear were the sounds of the tiny rain drops. **To know that Our Lady was right there just a few feet from me was the most wonderful, comforting, exciting thing that has ever happened** to me. I get chills every time I think of that night. No, I did not see her, but I knew she was there! This time, I did not question anything. That night changed the entire course of my life and those of my loved ones.

I arrived home from Medjugorje about 1:00 a.m. and was completely exhausted and went straight to bed. However, I was unable to sleep and woke up at 5:00 a.m. and decided to take a long, hot shower. While standing there I heard a tiny voice that seemed to come from within say, *"You are a bridge."* This had never happened to me before, and I remember laughing and thinking that I was experiencing jet lag. "How can a person be a bridge?" Then it all seemed so clear. I was a Protestant, yet I believed everything with all my heart. It wasn't the things that I could see that had strengthened my faith, but the things I didn't see. Many Catholics still do not believe in Medjugorje. I went to see with my own eyes and came back convinced that everything was real. It did not matter what religion you were as long as you listened to her message of peace. She loves us all! We should never close our minds to anything, for if everyone could cross the bridges we would indeed have peace.

One month later on Thanksgiving night, November 26, 1987, I walked out onto my patio with my youngest brother Scott. He believed in God but was a complete skeptic as to the events in Medjugorje. There were seven of us talking about things in general when someone mentioned the word "Medjugorje". Scott was aggravated at hearing the word and challenged, "Okay, okay if the messages at Medjugorje are true, then I want to see a shooting star right there! " and he pointed to a particular spot in the sky. Kenneth said confidently, "Okay we can handle that. Let's ask

Mary for this specific sign." Now, I was very hesitant to do this because if nothing happened Scott would say, "See I told you!" I tried to tell them all, that this was not a good idea and you are not supposed to "test" God. I was completely ignored and we formed a circle joining hands. As Kenneth began the Lord's prayer, I was praying differently, "Please God, please show them this is all true." The two teenagers, my daughter, Katherine, and niece, Kristen, began giggling because other than "grace" on major holidays, we were not a praying family.

A mist suddenly formed around us as we joined hands, but I thought that it was fog, a common occurrence in Slidell. In the middle of the Lord's prayer, just about 10 to 12 seconds into the prayer, the two teenagers screamed, running into the house hysterically. Scott, my oldest brother, Sammy, Katherine and Kristen, all saw an unusually bright shooting star, (almost like a comet), in the exact spot that Scott had pointed to. My husband Ronnie, Kenneth and I did not see anything, as we were looking down praying with our eyes closed. We thought we could at least finish the prayer! I had to put a cold washcloth on Kristen's face convincing her not to be afraid. Scott seemed stunned! He admitted that he had asked for a very specific sign and received it immediately. He said that it wasn't only a star but it looked like a comet. He also said that the chances of that happening were probably a million to one and he had to believe it! Then we noticed something very strange. The thin mist that had formed around us a few minutes earlier was gone. It did not occur to me at the time that it could not have been fog as we were looking at stars. Our Lady was saying, "Believe in the messages of Medjugorje." It was a true miracle and a special gift for a yard full of Protestants.

My husband and children were greatly affected by my experience in Medjugorje because they knew I was not a person easily swayed. Kenneth entered an R.C.I.A. class immediately upon his return from Houston and was confirmed a Catholic at the next Easter Vigil Mass. However, we decided to stay Methodist, but began to fast and pray the Rosary. We were not convinced that jumping into the Catholic faith was the right thing to do. However, I worried constantly about this decision. Father assured me that we would not be going to hell because we were not Catholic. He advised us to allow time to go by and do what we felt was right. Every now and then we would find ourselves at Mass at St. Margaret Mary. It was my son Jeff who remarked, "Mom, don't you just feel better when you come out of St. Margaret Mary?" I prayed, "Lord tell us what to do. We are so mixed up." Shortly after this, the minister we were so fond of suddenly left the church, but we remained confused and hesitant. Was this a sign?

One Sunday, we were sitting in the back of St. Margaret Mary and a man approached us, inviting us to be gift bearers. We refused and explained that we were not even Catholic. He replied, "No", that he really wanted us to do it anyway. This seemed like an answer to our prayers and we knew we were destined to become Catholics. Although we knew it wasn't necessary, we felt unfulfilled until we made this major decision to join the Church. Sammy became Catholic at a service in New Orleans. Scott has remained a Protestant and we all respect and understand his feelings.

Mary is Our Mother, and I am sorry that it took so long for me to really know her. My only desire is that people of all faiths only open their eyes, their minds and lastly, their hearts to others, thereby respecting their fellow man for whatever their belief may be, as long as good evolves from it and not hate or persecution. If this story can open the heart of just one person, then I would be thrilled to know that I enabled someone to "cross a bridge," if only for a fleeting moment. If each of us could accomplish this simple task, the lasting peace Our Lady so desperately seeks would be a reality. It is not important what religion you are or even to travel to Medjugorje, because Medjugorje is anywhere you want it to be, even in your own backyard, as it was for us.

Chapter 7
SATAN - OUR REAL ENEMY

"I say to you who are my friends: Do not be afraid of those who kill the body and can do no more. I will show you whom you ought to fear. Fear Him who has power to cast into Gehenna after He has killed. Yes, I tell you, fear Him."
The Gospel of Luke 12:4-5.

The cross at Medjugorje is a SIGN to me. A few years ago, I had gone to Northshore Hospital and ran into someone I knew. She began telling me of her trip to Medjugorje and how she had seen the cross on the top of the mountain turn red, then gold. It then changed to the colors of a rainbow. It was a marvelous sign, and she turned to the people next to her to see if they had seen the sign. They saw nothing. The cross in Medjugorje, to me, is a sign! But NOT EVERYONE WILL SEE THE SIGN!

I believe our community has experienced enormous signs because the Holy Spirit obviously wants to use many of our parishioners, especially our youth, in a very powerful way.

I feel it is important to explain to parents and young people who are in our scripture program preparing for Confirmation, why this parish goes to such trouble to train them for Confirmation. We feel there are priests who would ask, "Why bother?" If you confirm in the eighth grade, then you would have nothing to worry about or programs to be concerned with. The Holy Spirit is supposed to do His work. A point of fact is that the eighth grade is not the best time in a young person's life to receive the Holy Spirit. These young people are simply not mature enough.

The reason that we got where we are goes back

to my sabbatical. The more I read about Our Blessed Mother's warnings and Paul's letter to the Romans, the more it became clear to me that one of the things we have to be concerned about is that all of us are up against the power of evil or the power of Satan.

Our own time seems to conform to the time in which St. Paul in his letter to the Romans talks about the "Wrath of God," or the "Day of the Lord." That era of time is going to be a frightening period. That is why it is important that the Holy Spirit be very real in the lives of all of us, particularly the young. This is what St. Paul says in Romans 1:16: "I am not ashamed of the gospel. It is the power of God leading everyone who believes in it to salvation,..."

You would weep if you knew how many people today, even who attend church, are ashamed of the Gospel or are ashamed of each of us. Paul goes on to tell us that this Day of Wrath will be a time of great unbelief. We know that since 1960, twenty-five percent of our Catholic people no longer go to church on Sunday. What about the others? Do you know, for example, that in most parochial schools, many of the children don't go to Mass on Sunday? Do you know that many of the children who attend C.C.D. go to class in place of attending Mass? One of our religion teachers was telling me recently that in his 4th grade C.C.D. class, three-fourths of the children never attend Mass and their reason is: "We go to C.C.D."

There are many young people and many middle-aged people who not only do not believe in the Eucharist, but actually make fun of it. Not since the Protestant Revolt have we seen a time where the Eucharist, the Body and Blood of Christ, is held up to ridicule by those who pretend to be

Catholics.

What are some of the other signs that Paul warns us about? Paul says in Romans 1:21, "They certainly had knowledge of God, yet they did not glorify him as God or give him thanks;..." The words, "Giving Thanks" are used in the scriptures to mean the Eucharist.

There are millions of our Catholics who don't go to church or if they do go to Mass, they receive Holy Communion in the state of sin. One of our converts of last year called me to say how upset she was about the youth at Mass making fun of the Eucharist by talking and clowning around. What a tragedy!

Paul tells us in Romans 1:25 that, "...these men who exchanged the truth of God for a lie and worshiped and served the creature rather than the Creator--..." Did you know that in the United States, we spend six and one-half billion dollars just on records? A show recently made an interesting point. It was reported that one company, MTV, controls the majority of what can be seen on TV. More money is spent on records in this country than the gross national income of countries like Panama. On MTV, a member of a group called "Guns and Roses" thanked Satan for an award they received this year.

St. Paul tells us another sign will be unnatural sex. "Their women exchanged natural intercourse for unnatural,.... Men did shameful things with men, and thus received in their own persons the penalty for their perversity." (Romans 1:26-27) Scientists say the major reason for the spread of AIDS is homosexual behavior, and yet the gay lobby criticizes anyone who points out that perhaps we need to take God's message to heart.

St. Paul continues in Romans 1:29, "They are filled with every kind of wickedness: maliciousness, greed, ill will, envy, murder, bickering, deceit, craftiness." Did you see the movie about Wall Street? The main character said, "Greed is good." That's the message of the 80's that all our children grew up with. Paul also tells us, "They disobey their parents, they're senseless, faithless, heartless, and ruthless." These are some of the warning signs that Paul gives us that may in some way mirror the warning that our Blessed Mother is giving to us in Medjugorje.

Today, invoke the Lord. "The Day of Wrath" may be here. That is why it is so important for us to recognize that the Holy Spirit is acting in a very strong and powerful way in this community and in many other communities. This is why we need to take Confirmation for our youth seriously. At St. Margaret Mary we have 66 men and women who teach these confirmation groups.

Years ago, there was a priest, probably one of the finest chaplains of the Newman Club, who worked in Lafayette. Every young person he met, he would always ask the the same question, "Peanut, will you die for Me?"

On one of our retreats, I talked about this and when we were in Medjugorje, John Mire shared a beautiful testimony about those words, "Peanut, will you die for Me?" You can understand what it means if you imagine Christ addressing each of you. "John," "Mary," whatever your name is put it in here..."there is one thing I need to know." "What is it Lord?" you ask. "Will you die for me?" Jesus asks.

It is similar to the question Jesus asked Peter, "Simon, son of John, do you love me?" We are afraid to answer the question. If we say we love Him, then He will demand that we serve Him and that means carrying the cross. It means overcoming temptation. It means supporting one another in need. It means embracing one another and affirming each other. It's the cross!

Can you stand in front of your high school friends and be a witness for Jesus Christ? Our young people can. They stood up in our church in front of a thousand and twice said: "Let me tell you what the Lord has done in my life." Many of them shared the great things the Holy Spirit has done. This gift wasn't just for them. The Holy Spirit did it for all of *us*!

Until we can all learn to serve, until we learn to pick up that cross, our love is suspect. Picking up that cross is the hard part. As George Bernard Shaw once wrote, "It's the cross that bars the way." Lord, we'll follow you, like Peter, we'll follow you, if we stay on top of the mountain and see all the signs. But are we willing to go to Calvary? "Peanut, will you die for Me?"

The good news to me is that the Holy Spirit is using our young people in an incredible way. We've had three small children standing in front of the chapel at night seeing great signs in the sky. We had high school students in Florida, Mississippi, and in Medjugorje overwhelmed by signs. The Holy Spirit wants to give our youth powerful weapons to fight evil.

Now you know the problem. We are living in difficult times, perhaps even in the "Day of Wrath" predicted by St. Paul. We are living in an age of disbelief; we are going to be subjected to the power of Satan, but we have a great weapon-the **Holy Spirit**. The **Holy Spirit** will empower you to overcome evil and that grace will come if we receive the Sacrament of Confirmation prepared.

You will be prepared to receive the gifts of the Holy Spirit if you can truly say, "I know Jesus; I love Jesus; I want to serve Jesus." The power is yours for the asking. When you stand before the Bishop to be confirmed, Jesus will ask you one question, "Peanut, will you die for Me?"

Why are we going to all this trouble? The answer is clear! I am convinced that the power of the Holy Spirit will never be a vibrant force in the lives of our children unless three things happen. First all of us, not just the young or the middle-aged, but also the old; *must* come to know Jesus Christ. Now I know you may say, "I went to a Catholic school". I believe some Catholic schools today may be a sign of disbelief if they are not producing children or adults who believe in the Real Presence of Jesus in the Eucharist.

HOW DO WE COME TO KNOW JESUS?

We come to know him by STUDYING AND PRAYING OVER SACRED SCRIPTURE. Twenty years ago, I stood up in front of our community and asked, "How many people have read the entire Bible?" There were only two! They were both converts. But it's not simply reading the scripture. Coming to know Jesus means we look at the scriptures in terms of what Christ is saying to you in your life. Clearly, the Bible intends to teach us what Jesus says. That meaning is the same now as it was almost 2,000 years ago. But scripture sharing asks, "What is Jesus saying to me today?" We'll never know Jesus if we don't read scripture as prayer, asking Jesus, "What does this text mean in my life Lord?" This is what we do in Bible sharing.

Secondly, WE COME TO KNOW Jesus BY LOVING HIM! The Holy Spirit will never be as powerful as He can be until we love Jesus Christ and this is not easy. Jesus Christ Himself said it, "How can you say you love God if you hate your brother?"

We discover our love of Jesus when we come to love our sisters and brothers. Until we can find Him and love Him in the weakest, in the black, in the poor, we will never love Jesus Christ. That is why I was so thrilled this last year with our Embrace Group. Our young people began to understand just what the Holy Spirit wanted them to know; that in loving one another, they would find the very presence of Christ. We do this best in small communities, such as the sharing groups or retreats.

Do you remember what Jesus said? When you come to be judged, He'll ask you, "Why didn't you feed the poor, visit the sick?" You will answer, "I didn't know it was You."

You find Christ in one another by loving each other, and that's why the Mass is so important. That's why we can't allow it to be taken over by one or two people who are going to make a mockery of the Eucharist. The Mass has to be the sign for people who come hurting and know that someone is going to love them and care about them because we love Jesus. We can learn to love Jesus in our sharing groups.

Finally, **The Holy spirit Will Come In When You Learn To serve Jesus!** This may be the most difficult of our tasks. The cross is all about service to one another.

SATAN COMES TO SLIDELL

After one of our retreats, I warned our youth that Satan attacks our very beSt. The next day, I received a call from the parent of one of our retreatants asking me to come and bless their home.

I celebrated Mass in the home of this young woman, then I blessed the house. The father of this youth told me a rather chilling tale. About five in the morning, his daughter woke up, went to the bathroom and checked her clock. When she returned to her bed, she felt she had been freeze-wrapped. The bedroom, which was a converted garage turned into sleeping quarters, had become incredibly frigid. The daughter tried to pray, but the words would not come out, even the Our Father. Finally, the father was summoned. With tears in his eyes, he recounted how incredibly cold this room had become. "It was like walking into a deep freeze," he told me. Yet, there was no air conditioning in the bedroom and it was the middle of a hot summer.

When I shared this story a few months later at a priest's retreat, another pastor topped my story. "I went to bless a home in my parish," he began. "I was surprised that a second story bedroom was so frigid. 'Can't you turn off the air conditioning?' I pleaded with the owner. 'No Father, I can't. This room is always frigid,' she replied. I blessed the home, but I encouraged the owner to pursue the matter with the real estate people. Later, I learned that the previous owner had killed his wife in that room when he was discovered molesting his daughter. After killing his wife and then his daughter, he took his own life." The power of Satan is quite real!

New Age

Fr. LaFranz of the Center of Jesus The Lord, New Orleans, Louisiana told a group studying the New Age a terrifying tale. "A few years ago, I was asked to counsel a young man who had been involved in the occult from your area. The young person had been part of a Satanic ritual that involved killing a child and eating part of the heart. The man was never able to get over this gruesome act."

The New Age is a broad cover for different types of occult practices. The New Age has infiltrated into the Catholic Church itself.

In a Denver paper recently, it recounted how more adults are now claiming their parents practiced satanism. The Satan stories now number in the thousands. These accounts include animal sacrifice, cannibalism, and murder, all to honor Satan.

It is significant that many today in the Church discount the existence of Satan. I love the story told by Coach Dale Brown of LSU fame. According to the tale told by Brown, Satan was not pleased by the fact that so many people were going to Heaven, so he called a meeting of all the devils. "Tell them there is no hell," one devil suggested. "We have tried that," Satan responded. "Tell them there is no God," another devil suggested. "That's an old line," Satan said. But the smallest devil of all kept trying to get Satan's attention. Finally he was recognized. "Tell them there is plenty of time." "That's it! " Satan shouted, "We will tell them THERE IS PLENTY OF TIME." So if you wonder why so many people put off coming back to church, or going to confession, or forgiving one another, it may well be because Satan has convinced them..........THERE IS PLENTY OF TIME.

Pope Leo XIII, at the end of the 19th century, had a terrifying vision. He saw Satan and Jesus Christ. In their conversation Satan was told that he could use his power in the 20th century. This would be his century. So terrifying was this dream that the Pontiff ordered the recitation of the prayer to St. Michael after every Mass. This was discontinued after the Second Vatican Council.

ANGELS

Satan can be conquered by the intercession of our guardian angels and by the power of the Divine Mercy of Jesus Christ.

It is significant that Jesus refers to children having "Guardian Angels." In The Gospel of Matthew 18:1-2 Jesus was asked by the disciples, "who is of greatest in the kingdom of God?" Jesus said, "I assure you, unless you change and become like little children, you will not enter the kingdom of God." Jesus concluded this teaching by telling His followers, "'See that you never despise one of these little ones. I assure you THEIR ANGEL IN HEAVEN CONSTANTLY BEHOLD MY HEAVENLY FATHER'S FACE.'" The Gospel of Matthew 18:10.

I feel it is significant that angels have been seen in our parish church and chapel, both by an adult and a child. This is a reassurance to me that our parish is a prayerful place.

It was a disappointment to see in a widely used text for religious instruction the following statement: "Today, theology is restudying the whole question of angels and devils."(1) It takes a child-like person to believe in angels; but if Jesus and the

Bible said it, we should believe it.

[1] Anthony Wilhelm, *Christ Among Us*, 2nd ed. (New York: Paulist Press, 1975).

Chapter 8
LOYALTY TO THE POPE - THE LITMUS TEST

"I for My part declare to you (Peter), you are 'rock,' and on this rock I will build My church, and the jaws of death shall not prevail against it."
The Gospel of Matthew 16:18.33

I didn't want to include this chapter in the book. I delayed. It's such a risk. But I know this is the gift that the Holy Spirit must give us to become a Remnant Church. As I began to write in the chapel Saturday afternoon, I asked for a specific sign. Get George Knauer to invite me to supper, he has never done that before. A few minutes later, his wife Linda came over to me as she was beginning the Way of the Cross. "Would you like to have supper with George and me tonight?" she asked.

I had no choice!

The Catholic Church as an institution traces its origin to the first Pentecost. One of the integral elements of a Remnant community is loyalty to the Holy Father. This is the litmus test of belonging to Jesus Christ - the love and respect for the Pope.

Father Tim Deeter recently shared this insight about the Remnant Church. He was told recently by Father Jozo, a very holy priest from Medjugorje, that "A dark cloud is passing over the U.S. The Church in the west will be in schism (doctrinal error) and you must prepare your people to know their faith and be grounded in their true faith, so that when the day of tribulation comes, Catholics who want to practice the true faith may come to your parish as a place of refuge."

Our loyalty to the Pope is based on a promise

made to St. Peter by Jesus, "... you are 'Rock,' and on this rock I will build my Church,..." (The Gospel of Matthew 16:18) It was to Peter that Jesus gave the power to "bind and to loose", i.e. the power to forgive sins. Peter is always listed as first among the apostles in the New Testament. Even when the apostles argued over who had a right to the highest place in the kingdom, it was Simon Peter who was chided by our Lord Jesus, "Simon, Simon! Remember that Satan has asked for you, to sift you all like wheat. But I have prayed for you that your faith may never fail. You in turn must strengthen your brothers." The Gospel of Luke 22:31-32

Even St. Paul, who vigorously disagreed with Peter over the issue of circumcision of converts, acknowledge Peter's Primacy. Paul tells us that Jesus appeared to Peter first, even though we know Peter was not the first to see Jesus after the Resurrection. Peter was not first in the chronological order but first in the order of faith.

As a young student, I was thrilled to read of the death and burial of Peter in Rome. According to tradition, Peter was crucified upside down and buried outside the walls of Rome in what is now Vatican City. Archeologists, a few years ago, have found Peter's tomb directly under the main altar of St. Peter's Basilica. The original church of Constantine, built in 325, was filled in and the present church built over it. Peter's grave is marked with simple words in Latin that mean, "Here lies Peter."

It was easy growing up Catholic as a child under a Pope everyone considered a saint, Pope Pius XII. In 1950, it was this saintly man who wrote to all the Bishops in the world asking if they believed the teaching that Mary was assumed into heaven. When he received unanimous testimony worldwide, this Pope defined and declared that Our Blessed Mother Mary was assumed into heaven. This is a clear infallible teaching ex Cathedra; the first definition since 1870 defined infallibility that cannot be contested.

What caused the change among Catholics, priests included, from reverence and respect for the Holy Father and his opinions, to the state we are in today? It seems that there was a geophysical change. The Pope, after 1965, was no longer viewed as "God's mouthpiece." Two main issues caused Catholics to question Papal authority. The first issue was the marriage of priests.

Shortly after Vatican Council II, approximately 1967, Edward Schillebeeckx, a prominent Catholic theologian at the council addressed a huge crowd at Dominican College. "Religious Priests," he said, "would remain celibate. But secular priests would soon be allowed to marry."

As a young priest who was already feeling the weight of the cross of the priesthood, I, like many others, was overjoyed. The loneliness of the priesthood was already a tremendous burden.

However, in the synod of the priesthood in Rome, 1970, a married priesthood was not even considered. A few years later, married men were accepted as Deacons. Deacons are considered members of the clergy. Since then, Protestant ministers who converted to the Catholic Church were ordained as Catholic priests and remain married. Currently, there are more than 70 such men in the United States.

The clergy reaction was revolutionary. 100,000 priests world wide left the ministry. Devotion and loyalty to the Pope waned among many clergy. Even scripture seemed to conspire against the Pope. Jesus Himself had said, "Would one of you hand his son a stone when he asks you for bread?" Many priests answered the Holy Father, the Pope who refused to lift the weight of celibacy. Celibacy became the stumbling stone instead of spiritual nourishment.

The other main issue was contraception. Prior to 1960, theologians accepted as normative that birth control was intrinsically sinful. In 1960, Dr. John Rock, a Catholic from Harvard University, invented the famous birth control pill. Catholics were elated. Finally, there was a Catholic solution to contraception.

Pope John XXIII called a Papal Commission on contraception to study the pill and other forms of contraception. After his death, Pope Paul VI continued the work of these experts. Their conclusion, though not unanimous, was that contraception was not intrinsically evil. The Papal study was never officially published. Pope Paul wrote an encyclical, *Humanae vitae*, once again reiterating the Catholic position that all forms of contraception were intrinsically evil.

It was said that at least 25% of Catholics in this country stopped going to church on Sunday. They, like many priests, no longer believed that the Pope was "God's mouthpiece." "That's just his opinion," was a common reaction. Catholic consciences were often made up irrespective of Church teaching, and loyalty to the Pope grew weak among many.

What have been the results of this massive refusal of Catholics to accept the authority of the Pope, both in the area of marriage of priests and contraception?

We have already seen 100,000 priests leave the ministry. Homosexuality and sexual problems of the clergy surfaced. Many religious orders of women disintegrated. They no longer saw celibacy as a meaningful sign, and the aging clergy and nuns are an obvious result. The accusation concerning pedophilia among the clergy has been a national disgrace.

Thirty year ago, priests were arguing that contraception should be moral in the case of danger to the life of the mother or grave financial hardships.

Now contraception is viewed even by many Catholics as a right of women in any circumstances. Large families, once pride seen in being Catholic, are now viewed as abnormal even by loyal Catholics.

The question in the minds of many were not morally right or wrong. Sexual morality ceased to be a concern of many Catholics. Because of the side effects, they have lowered the amount of estrogen in the present birth control pill. As a result, some women will ovulate while on the pill even though they won't get pregnant. This means according to many experts that the BIRTH CONTROL PILL TODAY CAN ACTUALLY BE ABORTIVE. Without realizing it, many women may have involuntary abortions. The worst is soon to come. The French pill recently developed is now an easy way to have an abortion. It will soon be available in this country.

Children in many public schools are given free condoms and told to be "safe."

Abortion is now approved by the majority of Americans. What impact did the faith of 60 million Catholics have on the abortion debate? Precious little. Abortion condemned by the early church is embraced by many major Catholic politicians. Too few Catholics speak out publicly about the evil of abortion.

Materialism in priests, nuns and lay people alike is a major spiritual danger. Material good replaced prayer in the lives of priests and religious and children in the lives of the laity. The average priest and religious watches three times as much TV as he or she prays. The divorce rate among Catholics became epidemic.

After we see some of the ill effects of failing to "agree with the Pope," we can say we should have listened and obeyed him.

The importance of this loyalty to the Pope cannot be emphasized enough. Loyalty to the Pope will be the "Litmus Test" in the time of trials for the Remnant Church. Clearly, Pope John Paul II is under the direct protection of Our Lady. When he was shot in St. Peter's square at point blank range, he should have been killed. But just as the gunman pulled the trigger, the Pope leaned over to look at a picture of Mary on a child. Josyp Terelya, the prophet from the Ukraine, claims the Pope will face another assassination attempt in 1995. Following a time of great trials, Russia will be converted and peace will occur. It is a conviction that I have that only those communities loyal to the Holy Father will be under the mantle of Mary and become the Remnant Church.

But how do we get there from here?

I have shared many times with my community

the pain I experienced by not having my own little girls. This is the price we pay, since priests are not allowed to marry in the Catholic Church. Yet, I have been rewarded by the love of countless children. Surrender by those who disagree with the Pope either on clerical celibacy or contraception is the only answer. I have no magic argument to prove the Pope is right and you are wrong.

I know the answer lies somewhere in the total surrender of your will and mine to Jesus Christ through our Blessed Mother. St. Louis de Montfort tells us the perfect path to perfection lies in a total surrender of self to Jesus through Mary. That surrender includes even my arrogant strong will and yours.

St. Ambrose in the fourth century wrote, "Where Peter is, there is Christ." I still wish it were 1967 and I were 35 and free to marry as a Priest. But like those troubled with the issue of contraception, I know the act of surrender is an act of the will. I choose to be under the umbrella of Peter. Yet this flies in the face of my feelings.

Those of you who are faced with the issues of birth control and abortion will one day soon be given the same kind of choice - your own opinions and feelings or surrender.

The gift of the Holy Spirit I pray for each of you is that of total surrender to Jesus through Mary. Only then will you be under the umbrella of Peter.

The remnant will be small because loyalty to the Pope involves obeying him even when we don't feel like doing so, or think we know better. But when the cross seems the heaviest, you must remind yourself that loyalty to the Pope will be the final "Litmus Test" of a Remnant Church. May the

Holy Spirit give each of us that gift to try to do what we are told even when our feelings rebel. Every time we pass our church, the Cross of Jesus will remind us that surrender is never easy!

You recall the vision of St. John Bosco, a Pope who looks quite like the present pontiff is steering the ship of the Church through dangerous waters. There are two lights that illumine his way; Our Blessed Mother and the Eucharist. (See Back Cover)

It is obvious that the Holy Father is integral to the final plan of the Triumph of the Immaculate Heart of Mary. Pope John Paul II is her man. The glory we await will take place on his watch. It is important to know that loyalty to the Pope will be the "Litmus Test" of a REMNANT COMMUNITY.

Chapter 9
TOTAL CONSECRATION TO JESUS THROUGH MARY

"In turn He said to the disciple, 'There is your mother.' From that hour onward, the disciple took her into his care."
The Gospel of John 19:27.

On December 8, 1992, hundreds of parishioners of St. Margaret Mary made the Total Consecration at every Mass. St. Louis de Montfort recommended the Total Consecration to Jesus through Mary as an effective means of spiritual growth.

In order to prepare our parish for this consecration, I sent out the following letter on October 1, 1992:

Dear Parishioners,

On May 13, 1917, Our Lady began appearing to three children in Fatima, Portugal. Lucia (10), Francisco (9), and Jacinta (7), were visited by a lady in white. "I am from Heaven," she explained.

Mary appeared on the 13th of the month for the next five months. Our Lady emphasized the recitation of the rosary to end the First World War. She showed them a heart pierced with thorns. "Jesus," she said, "wishes to make use of you to have me acknowledged and loved. He wishes to establish in the world the devotion to my Immaculate Heart....My Immaculate Heart will be the refuge and the way that will lead you to God."

Our Lady gave them a vision of Hell. The groans of pain and despair they heard horrified them and made them tremble. The children had been prepared for this momentary visit to hell since

Mary had promised they would go to Heaven. To save poor sinners, God wanted to establish devotion to her Immaculate Heart. Then Mary made a prediction, "If what I say is done, many souls will be saved and there will be peace. The war is going to end; but if people do not cease offending God, a worse one will break out during the pontificate of Pius XI. When you see night illumined by an unknown light, know that this is the great sign given to you by God that He is about to punish the world for its crimes by means of war, famine, and persecution of the Church and of the Holy Father."

The Blessed Mother went on to request the consecration of Russia to her Immaculate Heart and communion of reparation on the first Saturdays of the month. "If my requests are heeded, Russia will be converted and there will be peace. If not, she will spread her errors throughout the world causing wars and persecutions of the Church. The good will be martyred, various nations will be annihilated. In the end, my Immaculate Heart will triumph. The Holy Father will consecrate Russia to me, and she will be converted and a period of peace will be granted to the world."

The final apparition took place October 13, 1917. Seventy thousand people gathered. It rained constantly. Early in the afternoon, Lucia and her two cousins were in ecstasy. The clouds parted, and Lucia saw a lady dressed in white with Saint Joseph holding the infant Jesus. Then Lucia saw a sorrowful Mary and an adult Jesus who looked with pity on the crowd and raised His hand to bless the pilgrims. At the end of her ecstasy, Lucia saw Mary as Our Lady of Mount Carmel dressed in dark brown.

For ten minutes, the Sun danced like the fire

wheels in Ezekiel, spinning and throwing off rays of different colored light. The Sun then began to plunge to the earth. People screamed that it was the end of the world; then the Sun returned to its place and everyone was completely dry.

Two of the cousins died - Francisco in 1919 and Jacinta in 1920 of the flu epidemic. In 1939, a great light appeared in the skies over Europe. Lucia knew the Second World War was soon to begin. Shortly afterwards, Hitler invaded Austria and the great war began.

Lucia, who is now a Carmelite nun in Portugal, was given a third secret that was to be divulged in 1960. The written message was sent to the Vatican to be opened by the Holy Father. Many believe the time of tribulation or trials throughout the world that had been predicted by our Lady and the great loss of faith are key components of the third secret. This third secret has been read by the Popes, but the contents have never been officially divulged.(1)

In order to prepare for our Total Consecration, we will begin with the 75th anniversary of the final apparition at Fatima on Tuesday, October 13, 1992. We will have the rosary at 6:00 p.m., followed by Mass at 6:30 p.m. After Mass we will have a documentary on Fatima that will last a half hour.

In order to make the total consecration to Jesus and Mary, you must begin the prayers on November 5. The private prayers are recited for 33 days. On December 8, we will make the Act of Consecration at every Mass.

I have purchased the two pamphlets for anyone wishing to make this Total Consecration. If you did not sign up Sunday and wish to get these books, please call my office. These will be a gift from the parish to you.

The motto of our Holy Father, Pope John Paul II is, "Totus tuus". These words which are emblazed over the letter M means "totally yours." The M stands for our Blessed Mother, Mary. In summary, this is what Total Consecration means - that we belong totally to Mary. As we consecrate ourselves to Mary, we also consecrate ourselves to Jesus Christ. Devotion to Mary always brings us to Jesus. If we totally commit ourselves to Mary, we likewise commit ourselves to Jesus. Incidentally, the present pope has made this consecration and renews it daily.

There is a battle taking place between good and evil. In The Remnant Church the children of Mary will flock to be under her protection. In Revelations 12:1, we are told, "A great sign appeared in the sky, a woman clothed with the sun, with the moon under her feet, and on her head a crown of twelve stars." The scene depicted in our window in the chapel stands for the TRIUMPH OF THE IMMACULATE HEART OF MARY. Satan will be conquered and Jesus will use His Mother as a powerful instrument in his Hands to defeat the evil one.

You will notice in that same chapel window that there are two angels. One of the angels will remind us of Katie Hernandez, the child who recently died. She stands for every VICTIM SOUL, young and old in our parish. One of the angels will have only one wing. This is to remind us that all of us are flawed, WE ARE ALL ANGELS WITH ONLY ONE WING. By ourselves we cannot fly but together we can soar. May you always be under the safe protection of Our Blessed Mother.

Nearly 400 copies of the pamphlets, *Total Consecration* and *Catechism on True Devotion* were distributed. Incidentally, one of our youth leaders shared this story with our confirmation retreat team. During the Thursday night prayer meeting for young adults, a woman got up and began to cry, "I saw the Archangel Michael during the Mass" she said, "He was dressed in Gold."

REQUIREMENTS

The exterior practices of "Total Consecration" include a 33 day preparation as outlined by St. Louis de Montfort in his Treatise. Secondly, the recitation of the Little Crown of the Blessed Virgin, composed of 3 Our Father's and 12 Hail Mary's in honor of Our Lady's twelve privileges. Third, the wearing of a little chain or medal. This is to remind us of our slavery to Jesus in Mary. You are also expected to have very special devotion to the mystery of the Incarnation, a great love of the rosary and the recitation of the Magnificat.

The interior practices of this consecration consists in doing all your actions THROUGH MARY, WITH MARY, IN MARY, AND FOR MARY, IN ORDER TO DO THEM MORE PERFECTLY, THROUGH JESUS, WITH JESUS, IN JESUS, AND FOR JESUS. In other words, it means that we must live our daily lives in union with Mary.

At the end of the 33 days of preparation, it is recommended that prior to making the "Total Consecration", one should go to confession and Holy Communion with the intention of giving oneself as a slave into the hands of Mary. Once a year this consecration should be renewed.

Consecration To Jesus Christ The Incarnate Wisdom, Through The blessed Virgin Mary! (Formula)

O' Eternal and Incarnate Wisdom! O' sweetest and most adorable Jesus! True God and true man, only Son of the Eternal Father and of Mary always Virgin! I adore thee profoundly in the bosom and splendors of Thy Father, during eternity; and I adore Thee, also in the virginal bosom of Mary, Thy most worthy Mother in the time of Thine incarnation.

I give Thee thanks for that Thou hast annihilated Thyself, taking the form of a slave in order to rescue me from the cruel slavery of the devil. I praise and glorify Thee for that Thou hast been pleased to submit Thyself to Mary, Thy Holy Mother in all things, in order to make me thy faithful slave through her. But alas! Ungrateful and faithless as I have been, I have not kept the promises which I made so solemnly to Thee in my Baptism; I have not fulfilled my obligations; I do not deserve to be called Thy child, nor yet Thy slave; and as there is nothing in me which does not merit Thine anger and Thy repulse, I dare not come by myself before Thy most holy and august majesty. It is on this account that I have recourse to the intercession of Thy most holy Mother whom Thou hast given me for mediatrix with Thee. It is through her that I hope to obtain of Thee contrition, the pardon of my sins and the acquisition and preservation of wisdom.

Hail, then, O' Immaculate Mary, living tabernacle of the Divinity, where the Eternal Wisdom willed to be hidden and to be adored by angels and by men! Hail, O' Queen of Heaven and earth, to whose empire everything is subject which is under God. Hail, O' sure refuge of sinners, whose mercy fails no one. Hear the desires which I have of the Divine Wisdom, and for that end receive the vows and offerings which in my lowliness I present to thee. I, N. faithless sinner, renew and ratify today in thy hands the vows of my Baptism; I renounce forever Satan, his pomps and works; and I give myself entirely to Jesus Christ, the Incarnate Wisdom, to carry my cross after Him all the days of my life, and to be more faithful to Him than I have ever been before.

In the presence of all the heavenly court, I choose thee this day for my Mother and mistress. I deliver and consecrate to thee, as thy slave, my body and soul, my goods both interior and exterior, and even the value of all my good actions, past, present and future; leaving to thee the entire and full right of disposing of me, and all that belongs to me, without exception, according to thy good pleasure, for the greater glory of God in time and in eternity.

Receive, O' benignant Virgin, this little offering of my slavery, in honor of and in union with, that subjection which the Eternal Wisdom deigned to have to thy maternity, in homage to the power which both of you have over this poor sinner, and in thanksgiving for the privileges with which the Holy Trinity has favored thee. I declare that I wish henceforth, as thy true slave, to seek thy honor and to obey thee in all things.

O' Admirable Mother, present me to thy dear Son as His eternal slave, so that as He has redeemed me by thee, by thee He may receive me! O' Mother of mercy, grant me the grace to obtain the true Wisdom of God; and for that end receive me among those whom thou, lovest and teachest whom thou, leadest, nourishest and protectest as thy children and thy slaves.

O' faithful Virgin, make me in all things so perfect a disciple, imitator and slave of the Incarnate Wisdom, Jesus Christ thy Son, that I may attain by thine intercession and by thine example to the fullness of His age on earth and of His glory in Heaven. Amen" (2)

During a recent sermon, a seven year old child saw something rather interesting.

After Mass, the child told her mother that two angels had appeared during the sermon. One huge angel held up the cross which is on the back wall of the church behind the altar. The thing that most surprised the child was the huge diamond on the cross.

Total Consecration will be another tool in the hands of Our Lady to mold a community to become the Remnant Church!

[1]Alphonse Cappa, S.S.P., *Fatima Cove of Wonders* (Boston, MA: Daughters of St. Paul).

[2]*Preparation for Total Consecration: According to Saint Louis Marie de Montfort* (New York: Montfort Publications [1992]), 83-86.

Chapter 10
VISIT TO DENVER

"He then went up the mountain and summoned the men He Himself had decided on, who came and joined Him. He named twelve as His companions whom He would send to preach the good news;"
The Gospel of Mark 3:13-14.

In the last chapter, we discussed the Total Consecration of oneself to Jesus Christ through the hands of Mary. The individual becomes a slave of Jesus and Mary. St. Louis de Montfort calls it a perfect renewal of one's Baptismal vows.

You recall that at the wedding feast of Cana, Our Lady gave the stewards an admonition, "Do whatever he tells you." The Gospel of John 2:5.

I have never met a couple who have so perfectly carried out this Total Consecration as George and Linda Knauer. This couple moved to Slidell about five years ago. Linda was not a Catholic at the time; George was a fallen- away Catholic. He had been involved in a previous marriage bond and sought to have the marriage annulled. Linda attended the R.C.I.A. convert instructions with George. She was received into the Catholic Church in 1990. One year later, after George received his annulment, they had their marriage blessed at St. James Church in Medjugorje by Father Ken Harney, the associate pastor of St. Margaret Mary. From that moment, their spiritual life seemed to have taken wings.

George and Linda were members of the Teams group to which I belong. They revived my interest in the Total Consecration in September of 1991. I had read St. Louis de Montfort's book *True Devotion to Mary* as a young student. However, it was well over my head at the time. On my retreat the following month, I decided to make the consecration, which I did on December 8. In great measure, it was the encouragement of George and Linda, that all the members of our Teams group made the Total Consecration.

It is one thing to make the Total Consecration. It is far more difficult to live it. George and Linda decided they were being called by Our Lady to open a retreat house in Denver. Josyp Terelya had been told at the Mother Cabrini Shrine by Our Blessed Mother that this place would become the major site for her apparitions in the Americas. What could have caused George and Linda to make decision to give up their jobs, which brought them more than $100,000 a year and leave Slidell?

On October 14, 1992, I visited George and Linda in their new ministry. They had moved a month earlier to Golden, Colorado, about ten minutes from the Shrine of Mother Cabrini.

In the course of the meal, I had the opportunity to get George and Linda to share with us what motivated them to make this difficult decision to serve Our Lady so completely. It was obvious from our conversation that the house they now occupy really belongs to Mary. This couple would provide not only meals and lodging but minister to any guests who would come to visit the Shrine of Mother Cabrini.

It was now George and Linda's turn to tell us how Total Consecration had resulted in opening up of Harvest House," their retreat house.

"You and Linda tell us why you made this crazy decision to come here and open Harvest

House?" I said. The conversation went like this:

George: "We'll, let Linda..."

Fr. Carroll: "Now, this was a crazy decision. George was the Head of the Department of Oceanography at the University of Southern Mississippi, and you were a high powered computer expert. Why did you make this move?"

Linda: "Why did we do this? We've been, of course, going through a pretty significant change over the past three years, since our first trip to Medjugorje in September, 1989. However, this particular saga started sometime in May of this year.

"On the third of May, George stopped me as I was going out the door to our chapel for Perpetual Adoration to ask to me to pray about what we should do. He was becoming more discontented with his work (although externally hehad never been in better shape professionally). He said he was just getting fed up with science. He didn't believe in it anymore and needed a God career; we both needed God careers. He'd asked me to pray about it a couple of times before. So I went to the chapel and was praying before the Blessed Sacrament. As I asked about our work, I saw an image of part of a house and the concept of a bed and breakfast was infused, and it was given to me as in pictures with the windows like these (she pointed to the windows in her new dining room). I felt the room had windows on two sides where people would sit for their morning coffee. Since our dining room does not have this configuration, we feel that we will replace the bunje jump (the bunje jump is a comic reference to double doors off our kitchen, which opens to an empty space one story above the ground), with a room like in my vision, as soon as Mother Mary sends money. In any case, it was like I completely understood this concept as a sort of Medjugorje experience: people, families going on pilgrimages, having a place to stay as a base. You go, do your prayers, but you're on retreat. You're not trying to figure out the activity of the day, you're not trying to figure out whether we should go to McDonald's or Burger King. We would take care of all that for the pilgrims. Let them use their time for the prayer experience."

Father Carroll: Just a few years ago, Linda was not Catholic and after returning from her first trip to Medjugorje, decided to enroll in the R.C.I.A. class. It was during this period that she decided to enter the Church. George was in an invalid marriage and was able to get an annulment and then their marriage was blessed in Medjugorje, during their 4th trip."

Linda: "And what a blessing through the good offices of Father Harney, our associate pastor, we were able to have the ceremony and Mass in the room of apparitions." (i.e. where the six visionaries had their apparitions during the early years)."

Father Carroll: "....then she just took off and became the most prayerful woman that you can imagine."

George: "Yeah, she even started wearing a scarf like the little old ladies in Medjugorje . . . I call her, 'little babushka.'"

Linda: "When I came back from praying in the chapel, George and I talked and I told him what had happened. We went for a walk and we kept accumulating this idea. Seems that George had also been chewing on a similar idea. Now as I look back, I think the experience of discerning just what we were suppose to do is very similar to anyone's faith experience, or growth experience. It kind of goes like, 'I can do anything, I'm suppose to do and only I can do this! ' And then it changes to 'no, no, no I can't do any of it. We don't have the money. What about our jobs? What about our retirement, our medical insurance, etc?' How do you evaluate whether your thoughts are valid or whether it's some kind of deception? Well, one of the first things we did was to ask our prayer team to pray about this for us. No sooner said than done. One of our prayer team members, Judy Campbell, again in front of the Blessed Sacrament, (remember a remnant community is a prayerful community) was led to the Gospel of Mark 3:13-14. "He went up the mountain and summoned the men He himself had decided on, who came and joined him. He named twelve as his companions whom he would send to preach the good news;" I note here that the Cabrini Shrine is on a mountain and that St Louis de Montfort describes Our Lady's cohort as 'Apostles, of the Last Times'. Anyway, on May 24th, George wanted to check this reading in his Bible. He found both bookmarks at that passage. It was beginning to sound like 'The Twilight Zone.' On May 25th, we opened at random the book of messages through Fr. Gobbi, to paragraph 414J where Our Lady calls for Apostles of the Last Times. Interestingly and moving right along, I was coming to this area for the first time in my life for a family reunion. So I said, 'Great, I'm going to get to the airport a day early and if we are really supposed to do this, Mary's going to point out the house using a pillar of cloud and I'm going to buy it.'"

George: "And I even thought that Mary might actually do such a thing, so I gave her power of attorney."

Linda: "Actually, even though I was prepared to act

in case I was led immediately to a house, it really didn't work out that way. But I'd better back up a bit because in order to discern this, I'd had a number of infusions while sitting in front the Blessed Sacrament that I won't bore you with here. So, it was like Jesus asked me, 'What's it going to take to convince you?' Being a proper Protestant I said, 'it has to be scripture.' I was no longer a Protestant at the time, but it's almost automatic. Then according to Catholic teaching, I also said someone else should help discern this. Not just me. So, He (Jesus) sent me off to read scripture by opening the Bible at random. When I came to do these readings, there were twelve readings all having to do with buildings, lodging, or time scales. Incidentally, the final reading was in 1 Kings referring to Mount Carmel (that mountain word again) which paralleled similar prompting that I had eight years ago when George and I were still in California. This was to say the least, another powerful confirmation to me. Anyway, there was so much in the readings about lodging, etc., that I thought the whole Bible was about Harvest House. But as I said, the final reading was the same final reading as I had eight years ago in a different Bible. That to me anchored that experience. I knew that the California reading had come true because it had told me what to look for (blue and purple flowers) and where to go to look (Carmel mission) and I did it and the flowers were there, so that anchored that reading.

George: "Actually, the monastery in Carmel California (we were living nearby in Monterey) is where Fr. Junipero Serr evangelized so many Indians."

Linda: "And also where He is buried. It was at his sarcophagus where I found the flowers."

George: "So she got the same reading again in Louisiana. Our Lady now wants us not only to move to Colorado but to evangelize."

Linda: "But I had also asked for confirmation through someone else and that is where one of our parishioners from St. Margaret Mary, Ginger Nyberg, came in. She just happened to be out here (Golden, Co.) for her 25th wedding anniversary and received a locution for us at the fourth station at the Cabrini Shrine; the fourth station is a particular favorite of mine. Her locution went like, 'George and Linda, you belong here. Your work is here. You have planted your seeds in Slidell. Now move on quickly. I'm preparing the way for you.' Without Ginger being aware of it, I had come to realize we were indeed talking right now. For example, one of my directed readings had literally said the 24th day of the 9th month (Linda and George completed the purchase on their new house on Sept., 24, 1992) so I intended to work toward leaving Louisiana around the third week of September. At work the following day, a friend told me she was moving to Chicago and would be picking up her piano which I was keeping for her during the second week of September! I started grinning; I'm sure she thought I was nuts. But I just figured Mary was clearing the way for us. It clearly was not going to be 1993, but right now! "

"So I didn't find the house the first trip. I came home and two weeks later, George and I flew out together, that was August 15th and we planned to join in the Feast of the Assumption celebrations at the Cabrini Shrine and reconsecrate ourselves to Our Lady through the de Montfort formula. We arrived on a Thursday and by the end of Friday, we had made an offer on a house. We went around with a real estate agent doing things in a very human fashion, since we didn't get the divine finger pointing out the house. But there were a series of confirmations associated with that particular trip in that very day, we had somebody who needed to hear from us, somebody who needed a witness. That was of course a wonderful experience. It hasn't happened since we moved here! Which is where the doubts begin to seep in. And the doubts did actually start, soon after my first trip when I thought I had a picture of how things were going to go and they didn't. I'm still not sure why some of those things have not yet been fulfilled or why they may not be true. I don't know yet. But in between these two trips, when I came back with some things not working properly, I went to our Church and was praying in front of the statue of Our Lady saying, 'What gives here? How do I get this discernment that I'm supposed to need, whether to make this big move or not?' I received a teaching which was that if I act in faith, there is merit in it; if I require certainty, there is no merit. So I said, 'Great, I will act in faith, I don't require certainty.' (George kept saying easy for you to say). How do I tell that it's not an evil or a wrong thing? I'm consecrated to Our Lady. She is going to take care of things, I need to trust in her. So the message was 'faith and trust'. To trust in her, to change my direction if I'm going the wrong way. So that was the theme from that point on, both George and I stepped out in faith. Actually, acquiring our new house was very simple (although the engineering report was kind of scary, but we continued to trust). Some of the big steps were taken care of for us. We sold our condo by showing it to friends only one time. And I add that selling property in Louisiana was not easy at that time, given all the job layoffs, etc. So all of the really big things were taken care of for us.

"Our last week in Slidell began with a test of faith in that the sale of our condo was going to be held up while our title was cleared. But the rest of the week was filled with confirmation. On Wednesday, the message through Fr. Gobbi, which was read at Our Lady's Cenacle, was entitled "Apostles of the Last Times." On Thursday, I went to the Queen of Peace bookstore and there were the real prayers of our parish, five or more women who are really devoted to Our Lady. When I came in, they started laughing. They broke down and told me they had been discussing the message about the angels marking the foreheads of the faithful and they discovered they could see crosses on each other! When I came in, they saw one on me I couldn't see theirs but later, as I was driving I looked into the rearview mirror and saw mine. Then Saturday, at our last Mass at St. Margaret Mary, Fr. Carroll called the parish to Total Consecration. People from Our Lady's Cenacle were in the vestibule handing out our favorite books. We found out later, more than 300 people signed up. That was the best going away gift!"

*Editors note: If you are interested in a retreat house which will accommodate up to ten near the Cabrini shrine contact:
George and Linda Knauer
Harvest House
100 Skyhill Drive
Golden, Co. 80401
303-526-5478

THE SHRINE OF MOTHER CABRINI

The next day, I went to the chapel at the Shrine of Mother Cabrini to concelebrate Mass.

After communion, I asked the Franciscan if I could say a few words. I told the small congregation that I may owe my vocation to the priesthood to Mother Cabrini.

In 1955, I was a third year student at Notre Dame Seminary. It was customary at the time in the major seminary that the students had to work on Wednesday afternoon or work on a Master's thesis. The first week I decided to work. We moved bricks from one end of the basement to the other. The next week, the Prefect told us we were going to move them back. He didn't like the new location of the bricks. That was enough to convince me to work on a thesis.

During my course of studies, I discovered that I had become blind in one eye due to an infection. Later in my training, my blood pressure reached the stroke zone. With less than a year and a half to ordination, I was dismissed from the seminary. I spoke personally with Archbishop Rummel, but he would not relent.

For five months I became a janitor at my parish school, St. James Major. The rector was so impressed by the fact that I had completed my work for a Master's degree, in addition to the other course work, that he eventually talked the Archbishop into taking me back into the seminary eight months later.

The thesis I wrote involved Mother Cabrini. Dave Hennessey, a popular police chief, was killed by Italians in New Orleans known to be members of the Mafia. The year was 1891. A popular attorney took a full page ad out in the morning paper inviting the city to a public meeting.

"Difficult times demand difficult solutions", he said. There were eleven Italian men arrested for the murder of Hennessey. The crowd became worked up and stormed the Treme Street Jail. They killed the entire eleven, shooting those they did not hang.

The mayor of the City of New Orleans was frightened that this would result in a riot. At the time, the Italians and blacks lived in the same ghetto. Therefore, the mayor wrote and pleaded with Mother Cabrini to establish a house in the city. Within a year, Mother Cabrini had established an orphanage and school for Italian children on Esplanade Avenue.

At the time that I wrote the thesis, 'WHO KILLA DE CHIEF?" I visited the orphanage. I was greatly moved by the presence Mother Cabrini had in New Orleans. I visited her room and marveled at her accomplishments. This was the closest I had ever come to the presence of a real saint.

As I look back at the tremendous number of priests that left the ministry since 1960, I now realize my illness was a great blessing. It caused me to value the priesthood far more than I would have if I had had no problems. Perhaps in her own powerful way, it was Mother Cabrini who interceded for me during these trying times.

Later, I would share with one of the nuns at the Shrine of Mother Cabrini the testimony that she left. On the top of the mountain, there is a large statue of Jesus. The base of the statue includes a glass enclosure with a statue of Mother Cabrini.

Under the name and title "Mater Francisca Xaverio Cabrini" are written the words "omnibus ornata virtutibus," which means "clothed with all virtues." Perhaps Mother Cabrini wanted us to discover one more key to the Remnant Church. We must live the Virtues.(2)

[1] J. Gary Kuntz, *Our Holy Mother of Virtues: Messages for the Harvest* (1992), 59.

[2] Editors note: The interview with Theresa Lopez found in the first two printings has been eliminated. You will find Archbishop Stafford's letter regarding Theresa Lopez, the "alleged visionary" on page 187 in this edition.

Chapter 11
A SPIRIT FILLED COMMUNITY

"When the Paraclete comes, the spirit of truth who comes from the Father -- and whom I myself will send from the Father -- he will bear witness on My behalf."
The Gospel of John 15:26.

I completed this book on the vigil of the Feast of All Saints day. The first reading for that feast is taken from Revelation 7:2-4. The part of the text that struck me immediately was, "Do no harm to the land or the sea or the trees until we imprint this seal on the foreheads of the servants of God."

It was as if I had read that text for the first time. My conversation with George and Linda Knauer, came back ringing in my ears.

Linda Knauer had told how a group of prayerful women who were in the Queen of Peace bookstore had seen a cross embedded in her forehead. It was the same cross these women had seen in their own foreheads. I later learned that these women had seen the cross on my forehead as well at a different time.

The sign of the cross in Revelation, is the final step before the angels ravage the land. The trials predicted by Our Lady in Akita Japan and Medjugorje, Yugoslavia are the same - a time of great testing.

St. Paul writing to the Ephesians says, "Do nothing to sadden the Holy Spirit with whom you were sealed against the day of redemption." Ephesians 4:30

In the retreats we have had with our youth for

the last three years, we always end by calling down the Holy Spirit. Each of us asks for some special gift. The gift that I have sought is that I might not be a barrier to the outpouring of the Holy Spirit. I would suggest that you consider making that same appeal to the Holy Spirit. May you remove any obstacle to the outpouring of the Holy Spirit in your community.

The primary role of the Holy Spirit is to sanctify or to make holy. When you celebrate the feast of ALL SAINTS DAY, you are honoring all those who are in heaven, gifted with that grace by the Holy Spirit.

As I reviewed my own life, I realized that I had been an obstacle to the power of the Holy Spirit working in this community. It involved the gift of healing.

Twenty years ago, I visited Father Cohen, a Jesuit priest stationed at Loyola University. I wanted to know more about the Charismatic Renewal, which had just started a few years earlier. Patiently, Fr. Cohen told me that if I started a Charismatic prayer meeting, I would encounter problems.

Despite his warnings, I began to get involved in the Charismatic Renewal. I was thrilled by the idea that the Holy Spirit was working in the Church again. True to his warnings, problems began to surface. George, one of our leaders died of cancer, and Bill was killed in a wreck. Some of our members left the Catholic Church and joined fundamentalist groups because they said they were not being fed spiritually.

But it was the death of a young employee of Delta Airlines that affected me the most. When we learned he had cancer, we began to pray for his healing. We knew that God wants to heal. But our prayers turned out to be worthless and I was left with a feeling of guilt when the young man died.

The lessons the Holy Spirit taught me about healing were painful ones. It was Katie's mother who showed me how to properly pray for healing. We ask for healing but always with the intention that we want what God wills.

I learned from the Holy Spirit that a failure to forgive effectively bars any grace of God. Before we can ever expect to be heard, we must forgive those who have hurt us.

As Fr. Jozo learned from Our Lady, we can never pray from the heart until we learn to forgive those who have hurt us.

It was in Medjugorje, that the Holy Spirit taught me another invaluable lesson. God heals our greatest needs. I went to Yugoslavia in 1987, hoping to be cured of my physical blindness. I promised Our Lady I would be her best salesman. But the Holy Spirit healed my broken heart that was overburdened. And that gift was immeasurably more valuable to me than the cure of my eyesight.

The Holy Spirit has taught me that He selects victim souls. In every parish there are individuals who suffer greatly. They are truly victim souls. Katie Hernandez was one of our victim souls. She suffered most of her four and half years of life. In the eyes of God, suffering born with courage has immeasurable value. Ted Besh, the Delta pilot who shared his testimony in an earlier chapter, is also a type of Victim soul. He, like Katie, has been called by the Holy Spirit for a special mission.

In every parish, the Holy Spirit selects victim souls, like Katie and Ted. It is a mystery why God allows bad things to happen to good people. It is part of His Plan for our salvation.

THE HOLY SPIRIT SELECTS THE WEAK

The Holy Spirit showed me that He still loves to "choose the weak to confound the wise." Father Gobbi, who has been one of Mary's special priest sons, is short, fat and ugly. As soon as I saw him, I knew he belonged to the Holy Spirit. Father Tardif wrote, "I am the donkey that Jesus rides into Jerusalem." We know that the Holy Spirit frequently chooses children to manifest His power. He is still choosing the weak to confound the wise.

The greatest miracles I have witnessed have involved healings that occur through the Holy Spirit in the Sacrament of Penance. It was a dramatic moment in Medjugorje for me to see a woman who had been sexually abused by her father, willing to forgive him after she went to confession.

In 1960, Pope John XXIII, prayed for an outpouring of the Holy Spirit. I believe his prayers have been answered in many of the movements in the church, the Charismatic Renewal, Marriage Encounter and the Cursillo movement. You can see the outpouring of the Holy Spirit in the revival in the love of scripture and the love of Jesus as manifested in Perpetual Adoration.

The vision I have for EVERY Remnant Church, IS EMPOWERMENT BY THE HOLY SPIRIT. We must first survive the trials which will soon be upon us. "'Who are these people all dressed in white? And where have they come from?' I said to him, 'Sir, you should know better than I.' He then told me, 'These are the ones who have survived the great period of trial; they have washed their robes and make them white in the blood of the Lamb.'" Revelation 8:13-14.

The greatest gift of our time from the Holy Spirit will be the gift of perseverance. We will learn to surrender to whatever is God's will.

The entrance window of our church, which is on the cover of this book, is a clear sign of a community that is empowered by the Holy Spirit. The window should remind you of the cross of Medjugorje that turns red and then gold. It is a simple, but eloquent message that our salvation comes from the cross of Jesus Christ.

In the center of the cross is a large white hoSt. The Remnant Church MUST BE A POWERHOUSE OF PRAYER. That begins with a dynamic devotion to the Sacred Heart and belief in The Real Presence of Jesus in the Eucharist. The hour a week in adoration is the major contribution many in our community are making so that we might become a Remnant Church.

The final gift of the Holy Spirit is EMPOWERMENT. I could see in a small way how He took my weak shattered ego and empowered me. With and the encouragement of Deacon Johnny, I have been able to pray over our youth on the confirmation and eighth grade retreats with our prayer team. The sight of seeing many of these young people surrender and be slain in the Spirit is a testimony to the willingness of the Holy Spirit to use the weakest of all.

I believe the Holy Spirit will use this community in a powerful way. He wants the youth of this parish to feel embraced and know they are loved. A day will come when this parish will be totally empowered by the Holy Spirit. I don't know if everyone will raise their arms in prayer, or even if many will speak in tongues. These are minor league gifts, but I do believe that others will say of this parish, "I want to belong to St. Margaret Mary community, because everyone from the youngest to the oldest feels loved and embraced."

When others say of us as they said of the early Church, "see how they love one another," you will know that the entire parish has been given over to the Holy Spirit. For Paul says of all of the gifts of the Holy Spirit, the greatest is love.

The Remnant Church will be those Catholic parishes that are truly Eucharistic, have a strong devotion to Our Blessed Mother and are SPIRIT-FILLED. They recognize Satan as the real enemy. The remnant communities will have strong devotion and love for the Holy Father, the Pope. Total Consecration will be a mark of endearment.

Chapter 12
THE ANGEL OF TRIUMPH

"...The Lord keeps faith; He it is who will strengthen you and guard you against the evil one."
2 Thessalonians 3:3.

"'See that you never despise one of these little ones. I assure you, their angels in heaven constantly behold
My heavenly Father's face.'"
The Gospel of Matthew 18:10-11.

In the second letter from St. Paul to the Thessalonians, the great apostle tells us how to prepare for the Second Coming of Jesus Christ. Paul was warning the early Church not to be terrified that the "Day of the Lord" is here. He tells us that two things have to occur before the conversion of mankind takes place, before the Second Coming of the Lord.

What are those two things? You can find the answer in 2 Thessalonians 2:3. "Let no one seduce you, no matter how. Since the mass apostasy has not yet occurred nor the man of lawlessness been revealed ..."

A strong argument could be adduced that mass apostasy has already occurred in many parts of the world. Only 6% of Catholics in France and 3% in Italy presently attend church today. Belgium, one of the most Catholic countries, has only an 18% attendance. The scary prediction of Father Tim Deeter was that the schism or breaking from the Catholic Church will soon occur in this country. We know that only 30% of American Catholics believe that the Eucharist is the Body and Blood of Christ, according to a recent study.

In 2 Thessalonians 2:8, St. Paul tells us about the other sign, "Thereupon the lawless one (Satan) will be revealed, and the Lord Jesus will destroy him..."

Scripture tells us that, "Your sons and daughters shall prophesy, your old men shall dream dreams, your young men shall see visions;" (Joel 3:1-2) I will share my vision with you. I believe Our Blessed Mother has a special plan for each of you. Perhaps the statue of an angel that appeared recently at our doorstep may be another sign. And that vision is this, that each of you will have a devotion to your GUARDIAN ANGEL AND THAT OUR LADY WILL SEND THE ANGEL OF TRIUMPH TO EACH Remnant Church.

I would love to see this prophesy fulfilled here in St. Margaret Mary community. And if it does we will need to have devotion to our own Guardian Angel; but most of all, we will need the power and protection of the ANGEL OF TRIUMPH.

For a few weeks, one of our older parishioners has been seeing angels during Mass. Recently a small child has been seeing angels during Mass. The visions of this child was quite interesting.

TESTIMONY OF A HELICOPTER PILOT

I have decided to share with you a little of the testimony of Alan Fries. As a helicopter pilot and retired military man, he isn't the type you would expect to have visions. Perhaps it is because of his child-like faith in Jesus Christ and his Catholic Church that this convert has been so gifted.

I shared Alan's story at a talk I gave in Mississippi. A woman came up to me after the talk, "Father, I see angels too," she told me. She seemed relieved to know that even though your friends might think you are crazy, our God has a great sense of humor, He seems to love to play with his children.

Cardinal Sangelo Sodano, a Vatican Secretary of State, comments on the existence of Angels in an article in the *Catholic News Service*, written by John Thavis. He stated, "The more we become simple like child, then the more we penetrate the mystery of faith.

"We thank the Lord for having placed guardian angels beside us." Cardinal Sodano said, "The Dogma of the existence of Angels introduces us to the wonders worked by God." Recently, the Vatican newspaper ran the text of Cardinal Sodano's talk given on Angels. It was entitled: "Guardian Angels Guide Us And Cheer Us On The Path Of Life."

Pope John Paul II a few years ago gave a series of talks on angels saying: "they do exist, and have a fundamental role to play in the unfolding of human events." The pope warned about the bad angels, "not to give in to their flattery."

The *New Universal Catechism* states, "From faith we know there are angels, even though materialists and rationalists of all times deny it."

For those of you who are truly child-like, I know you will enjoy this part of Alan Fries' story. Alan first saw angels at Fr. Ken's Mass on July 12, 1992. The next week, I offered the Sunday evening Mass. This is what Alan said he saw:

"... Father Carroll celebrated the 7:00 p.m. Mass. I had forgotten about what had happened the previous Sunday. Just a little into the Mass, I began to see images again, and I knew and remembered at the same time. They were back! This time, there weren't as many on the altar but when you, (Fr. Carroll), stood at the altar, I now noticed in addition to the two on either side of the altar, a third very tall Angel. I could not look at this Angel. Before, and even now as I looked around, I could look at the other Angels, yet try as I might, not this one. I could look at his body, but not his face. My first thoughts were ones of, "he's too terrible to look at." The word that came to me was, HORRIFIC. Inside, I was torn between being drawn to look at him, more like compelled, and yet saying to myself, 'I cannot, it scares me,' Yet it wasn't a sensation of fear, like being afraid. However, fear is the only word I can describe. Even now as I write this, my hands and body begin to shake from the memory.

"Then something really different happened. As you started reading the Gospel, I saw two baby angels at the foot of the podium where they stayed for the rest of the Mass. Around you were four other angels, two on either side and right behind you was this one which I still could not look in the face. This Angel followed you everywhere.

"Several times I was drawn to the baby angels and it seemed they made me laugh, as did several other angels. It seemed like they were having such good time. It made me giggle uncontrollably and Rosemary (his wife) asked me, 'What are you laughing at?' I could only respond with, 'If you could see what I see,' and I laughed again. Then came the Hosanna. There were angels all around the altar. Some were coming and going, through the ceiling and still the tall angel stood behind you. Then there appeared on either side of the altar, two more tall angels. I asked myself why and suddenly I knew. They had come to guard you and the

CONSECRATION. THIS IS THE PART OF THE MASS THAT THE BREAD AND WINE IS CHANGE INTO THE BODY AND BLOOD OF CHRIST.

"I looked around and could see angels all over the place and when I looked back at the altar this time, I could look at the face of the Angel behind you. It wasn't a horrific, ugly face. It was one of INCREDIBLE POWER. I had mistaken what I first saw and now knew these three angels were special. They were like a special protection for you and the Eucharist. As I looked at the Angel behind you it was as if he spoke to me. I don't remember any words. All I could do was cry, wring my hands and respond with a nodding of my head and say, 'Yes, Yes,' again and again.

"This happened all throughout the distribution of communion. I would go from laughing to crying and each time as I looked at him I nodded and said, 'Yes." I glanced around the church and saw many, many angels. Then I began to see angels walking up the aisles with the people for communion. At times, it was almost too much. All I could do is lower my head and sob.

"After communion, as you were purifying the chalice, I realized that the two tall angels who had appeared earlier were gone. It was as if they were no longed needed. However, the one that I first noticed with you was still behind you and stayed there even as you left. As Mass ended, the angels seemed to fade from view."

****

THE BLUE ANGEL

There is presently a blue angel in our prayer

garden. It was a timely gift. One of my secretaries who was particularly troubled asked God for a special sign. "Please send me a blue angel," she begged. Now we know that you are not supposed to ask for signs. However, God sometimes honors the requests of his children. Two days later, a blue angel appeared at our office.

For over a hundred years, angels have stood guard over some of the most beautiful young women in New Orleans at Holy Angels Academy. That high school is closing after all these years. A few months ago, I went to Holy Angels Academy and asked that if they had any left over statues of angels, I would love to have one for our children's prayer garden. Unexpectedly, this statue arrived at our church in Slidell. I believe this statue of a blue angel is a reminder that Our Lady promised she would send an ANGEL OF HER TRIUMPH.

Last year during a Marian convention put on by the Mir group, the priests who attended on Sunday were asked if they had a special devotion to their guardian angels. If enough of you do, I was told, we will have a public consecration to your Guardian Angel. Since I have caused my Guardian Angel such problems during my life, I said I would be glad to make the consecration.

The priests present who wished to do so publicly read their Act of Consecration led by Archbishop Philip Hannan. The Consecration prayer is as follows:

"Holy Guardian Angel, Who has been given to me from the beginning of my life as my guardian and companion.

"I, a poor sinner, (name), desire to consecrate myself to you before my Lord and God, my heavenly

Mother Mary, and all the angels and saints, I wish to unite myself closely to you forever.

"In this union, I promise always to be loyal and obedient to my God and Lord and to Our Holy Mother, The Church. I promise always to acknowledge Mary as my Mistress, Queen and Mother and to imitate Her way of Life.

"I promise to acknowledge you always, as my Holy Guardian and to promote, as much as lies in my power, the veneration of the Holy Angels as the protection and the help which is given to us in a very special way, in these days of spiritual combat, for the kingdom of God.

"I beg you Holy Angel of God obtain for me a love so strong that I may be inflamed by it. A faith so firm that I may never falter. I bet you to assist me against the assaults of the enemy.

"I beg you for the grace of Mary's humility, so that I may escape all danger and guided by you may reach the gates of our heavenly home. Amen."

Church Approval

The late Pope Paul VI, after he had studied the acts of consecration to Holy Guardian Angels, said: "The Opus Angelorum (Work of the Angels) is a great work of love for our brothers in the priesthood, it has an important missionary mandate in the Holy Church."

To consecrate ourselves to our guardian Angel does not mean that we make the angel the center of our life. It means: "that the Holy Angel, by virtue of this consecration radiates his light with greater strength into our souls; he makes us understand more clearly the realm of faith and we receive new joy in what we are trying to achieve and sanctify in our vocation." (1)

Prior to his death, Pope Pius XII, in his last homily said this: "We must be united with the holy angels, we must form with them a great and strong family, in view of the times which are coming upon us."

Conclusion

One of the pieces of the puzzle to understanding the Remnant Church IS DEVOTION TO OUR GUARDIAN ANGELS. It takes a very child-like person to do this. But remember the words of Jesus, "I assure you, unless you change and become like little children, you will not enter the kingdom of God." The Gospel of Matthew 18:2-3.

[1]*Christ To the World "The Work of the Holy Angels"* n.1 Jan-Feb.,1984 vol. XXIX; Vid Propaganda c-00187 Rome-Italy

For further information I would suggest you write to: Confraternity of Priests in
Opus Sanctorum Angelorum
P. O. Box 2146
Menlo Park, Ca. 94025

Missions Office
Casa Regina Pacis
2495 Fatima, Portugal

Chapter 13
FATIMA - A LINK TO THE FUTURE

"A great sign appeared in the sky, a woman clothed with the sun, with the moon under her feet, and on her head a crown of twelve stars . . . then another sign appeared in the sky: It was a huge dragon, flaming red, with seven heads and ten horns; on his head were seven diadems." Revelation 12:1;3.

"In the end my Immaculate Heart will triumph."
Message of Our Lady at Fatima 1917.

On October 13, 1992, our Remnant Church celebrated the 75th anniversary of the final apparitions of Our Lady at Fatima, Portugal. I realized that I had not put any emphasis on the Fatima story. It would be necessary to prepare our people for this celebration, so I wrote a letter to all of our parishioners inviting them to this anniversary celebration.

Why did so many priests neglect preaching the message of Fatima?

Perhaps we have to go back to 1960 to understand the dilemma many priests experienced. I was ordained a priest in 1959. I had grown up with a great love for Our Blessed Mother. In 1960, we were told the third great secret of Fatima was to be revealed.

I remember the tremendous numbers of confessions I heard as a young priest. Many suspected that the message would reveal a third world war or perhaps the end of the world.

The Pope read the Third Secret! A simple message was issued by the Vatican. "We cannot vouch for the veracity of the shepherd children," the terse announcement said. With that simple statement and the refusal to divulge this secret, devotion to Our Blessed Mother almost died in the Catholic Church.

THE FATIMA MESSAGE

On May 13, 1917, Our Blessed Mother began appearing to three children in Fatima, Portugal. Lucia, 10, Francisco,9 and Jacinta,7 were visited by a Lady in white. This was just over a year after they had been visited by an angel. The place was the Cova da Iria. The lady was even more beautiful than the angel, "I come from heaven" she explained.

Our Blessed Mother appeared on the 13th for the next six months. Mary explained the recitation of the rosary as a means of ending the first world war. "Jesus," she said, "wishes to make use of you to have me acknowledged and loved. He wishes to establish in the world the DEVOTION TO MY IMMACULATE HEART...My Immaculate Heart will be the refuge and the way that will lead you to God."(1)

We have already seen that Our Lady's warnings were not heeded. The second World War began, and communism began to flourish. As we listen today to the warnings of Mary in Medjugorje, we realize that even history could be changed if we listen to Our Lady.

As the Blessed Mother promised, Francisco and Jacinta soon joined her in heaven. Francisco died in 1919 and his sister in 1920. Lucia is still alive and living in a Carmelite Monastery in Coembra, Portugal.

Our Lady appeared to Lucia, the surviving

visionary, years later to give her permission to reveal the first two parts of the Fatima message.
First Secret

The vision of Hell, including Our Lady's promise to take the children to Heaven, the prediction of another war, martyrdom for Christians, persecution of the Church and the Holy Father.

Second Secret

The Devotion to the Immaculate Heart of Mary. Prior to this, Sister Lucia had kept this a secret.

In 1929, Our Lady came again. She asked for the Consecration of Russia to the Immaculate Heart of Mary and the Communion of Reparation on the First Saturdays. If men would fulfill her requests, Russia would be converted and there would be peace.(2)

This Consecration to the Immaculate Heart of Mary was done by Pope John Paul II on March 25, 1984. The Pope requested all the Bishops in union with him to make the Consecration. Although some say it has been properly done, several contemporary visionaries along with some long-time Fatima devotees, insist the consecration still has not been properly done and needs to be done again.

When asked why all the previous consecrations (made without participation of all the world's Bishops) had not sufficed, Lucia answered that Our Lord in 1929, insisted on the Collegian Act of Consecration (i.e. consecration of Russia by the Holy Father together with ALL the Bishops of the world) because: "I want my entire Church to know that this favor (the conversion of Russia) was obtained through the Immaculate Heart of My Mother so that it may extend this devotion of the first Five Saturdays LATER ON and put the devotion to this Immaculate Heart beside the devotion to My Sacred Heart."(3)

The third secret was never publicly revealed. This secret was written down by Sister Lucia and placed in an envelope and given to the Bishop of Fatima to be opened in 1960. The letter was sent to Rome and was read by Pope John XXIII. He decided not to reveal the contents.

On the night of January 25, 1938, an ominous red glow lit up the sky. It was seen in Europe and Africa and in part of America and Asia. Scientists called it an unusual display of the Aurora Borealis or Northern Lights. Sister Lucia knew it was the sign foretold by Our Lady. Several weeks later, Hitler invaded Austria and the Second World War began.

Our Lady's Requests At Fatima

1. Consecrate yourself to the Immaculate Heart of Mary.
2. Offer sacrifice for your own sins and sins of others.
3. Say the Rosary daily.
4. Make the five first Saturdays.
5. Visit the Blessed Sacrament in reparation for sins against her Immaculate Heart.
6. Do extra penances and say extra prayers for conversion of sinners.(4)

Incidentally, as we have seen earlier in this book "Total Consecration to Jesus Through Mary", as recommended by St. Louis de Montfort is an excellent form of consecration to Our Blessed Mother.

Five First Saturdays

To honor the Immaculate Heart of Mary and to make reparation for sins committed against her name, we were asked to make the five first Saturdays. What does this entail?
1. Going to confession.
2. Receive Holy Communion.
3. Recite five decades of the Rosary.
4. Spend 15 minutes meditation on the mysteries of the Rosary with the intention of making reparation.

The Third Secret Of Fatima

Officially, it is still a secret. When Sister Lucia delivered this hand written note to the Bishop of Fatima, she told him that it should be opened in 1960. "By 1960, things will be clearer," she told the Bishop.

Malachi Martin, in his book "The Keys of This Blood", speculates that the Third Secret contains the following:

1. A physical chastisement of the nations involving catastrophes, man-made or natural.
2. A spiritual chastisement, far more frightening for Roman Catholics, involving widespread lack of faith in many countries i.e., apostasy.
3. Russia is a key to the timetable.(5)

In a newspaper distributed by the Pittsburgh Center For Peace, entitled *Queen of Peace Special Edition II* quotes a letter from Sister Lucia written years ago to her nephew, a Salesian priest, Father Valinho. Sister Lucia wrote: "What I recommend to you above all is that you draw close to the tabernacle and pray. In fervent prayer, you will receive the light, strength, and grace that you need to sustain you and to share with others."

The same newspaper quotes the words of a modern day saint. Saint Maximilian Kolbe wrote, "Modern times are dominated by Satan and will be even more so in the future. The Virgin Mary alone, has received from God the promise of victory over Satan; in the glory of heaven, she needs our collaboration today. She seeks souls who will consecrate themselves entirely to her, becoming in her hands a force to conquer Satan and instruments to establish the Kingdom of God."(6)

On May 12, 1980, while at Fatima, Pope John Paul I said, "would you like me to tell you a secret? It is simple and after all, is no secret. Pray, Pray, much. Pray the Rosary every day."

The Chastisement

We have seen earlier that many prophetic voices have been raised trying to warn the world. Josyp Terelya, speaking in St. Margaret Mary Church, said without equivocation that this was the time predicted in the Book of Revelation. Our community was warned by Father Tim Deeter that schism would occur in the Catholic Church in the United States.

SISTER AGNES SASAGAWA

Our Blessed Mother appeared to a novice, Sister Agnes Katsuko Sasagawa, in a convent in Akita, Japan beginning in 1969 and ending in 1982. The events began when Sister Agnes was hospitalized. As Sister Agnes prayed her rosary, her guardian angel appeared to her to teach her a prayer that was new to her. This prayer is known as the Fatima Prayer: *"O My Jesus, forgive us our sins; save us from the fires of Hell; Lead all souls to heaven especially those most in need."* (*Of Your Mercy* is the usual ending.)

Sister Agnes began offering her intense sufferings for the conversion of sinners. She began to lose her hearing and by March 16, 1973, was totally deaf. On June 23, 1973, in adoration before the Blessed Sacrament, a brilliant light appeared. Sister Agnes saw many angels surrounding the altar in adoration of Jesus, truly present in the Eucharist. A very painful cross-shaped wound appeared on Sister Agnes's left hand.

On July 5, 1973, Sister Agnes's guardian angel led her to the chapel. Here she saw Our Blessed Mother. Our Blessed Mother told her that her deafness would be healed.

On July 6, 1973, all of the sisters noticed the wooden statue of Mary had a cross shaped wound in the right hand that was bleeding. Sister Agnes recalled the words of her guardian angel on July 5, 1973, *"The wounds of Mary are much deeper and more sorrowful."*

On October 13, 1973, the anniversary of "the miracle of the sun" at Fatima, Our Lady told Sister Agnes the following message: "If people do not repent, God will send a terrible punishment. It will be more severe than ever before, worse than at the time of the flood. A fire will fall from heaven and most of humanity will be destroyed and neither priests nor faithful will be spared. Survivors will be in such desolation that they will envy the dead."

Our Lady added that the only weapons left to you will be the Rosary and the Sign of My Son."

Our Blessed Mother added: "Satan would enter the Church with Cardinals opposed to Cardinals and Bishops to Bishops, Priests who revered Our Lady would be despised and attacked and church altars desecrated; and the Church would be filled with those who accepted a spirit of compromise. Satan would concentrate especially on attacking and deceiving consecrated souls."

The local bishop has made it clear that he believes there is an integral connection between Fatima and the apparitions in Akita, Japan. Mary, Our Mother, is obviously trying to warn us of the need to repent.

On May 30, 1982, Sister Agnes's guardian angel announced that through the intercession of the Blessed Mother, this pious nun would regain her hearing. Although she had been declared incurably deaf, she was miraculously cured.

On Easter Sunday, April 22, 1984, Bishop John Ito declared the events in Akita were supernatural in origin. In June 1988, through Cardinal Ratzinger, the Vatican declared the events in Akita were "reliable and worthy of belief."(7)

CHRISTINA GALLAGHER

Christina Gallagher, a young Irish housewife from Co . Mayo, is another important voice warning us of the coming chastisement. Although many of the messages Christina receives are especially for Ireland, her apparitions confirm the warnings that we have been given about our current age.

Chastisement

In a wonderful book entitled *Please Come Back*

to Me and My Son, R. Vincent sums up the messages Christina has received about chastisement:

"Many souls are being loSt. My Son's hand is about to come over the earth in justice. Please come back while there is still time. ... Tell all humanity. ... The Chastisement. ... The Purification is on the way. ... I love all my children. ... Repent. ... Unburden yourselves of all sin ... go to Confession, ... Receive My Son's Body and Blood worthily. ... Pray the Rosary, fast and make sacrifice. ... Show Christian love to all, even to persecutors."(8)

Suffering

Our Lady called Sister Agnes Sasagawa in Akita, Japan to become a victim soul. She endured great pain and so has Christina Gallagher. Christina has been led on the path of holiness to suffer as a victim for the conversion of sinners.

Ms. Gallagher considers her purpose in life is to pray and offer her sufferings for priests and religious, including the Pope, cardinals, and bishops, as well as for the conversion of sinners.

Christina has, like other visionaries, battled with Satan himself. The evil one has appeared to her in human form: half human and half animal. Christina was told by Our Lady that the Rosary is the most valuable protection and weapon in combating evil. She was also told that we must "pray the rosary from the heart".

Satan

Our Blessed Mother, in a message in August 1988, told Christina: ***The calamity has started.***

The influence of the Priince of Darkness is all around you. Arm yourself with My Rosary. My Church will be shaken, even its very foundation. My children who want to be saved must repent."

Our Lady went on to address those who don't believe in the existence of Satan. If people fail to believe in Satan, they deny the existence of sin and the need for Jesus as our Savior. Christina tells us, "You are to know about the existence of the Devil but not to dwell on it or worry about it but know that a **great battle is going on between God and the Evil One. We have no need to fear the darkness if we are in the light, if we permit and allow Jesus to live in our lives. That is the lesson I have been taught. The less I feared Satan and the more I trusted God, the more I was able to accept God's will."**(9)

SATAN EXISTS

All of us at one time or other have met individuals who don't believe in Satan. New Age philosophy has dulled the very concept of Satan in the minds of many. During the week prior to writing this chapter, a young couple visited my office.

I was preparing for my R.C.I.A. convert class on Thursday night. They begged to see me. Both Catholic, neither had gone to Church for some time. They had married outside the Catholic Church because of convenience.

The young woman shared a story of horror that happened earlier in the day. Her husband had left for work and she was still in bed. "Something got into my bed and started crawling around," she said. It was huge! It got into her and threw her out of the bed. It was the power of evil. She was unable to speak or cry out; she was petrified.

The young woman told how she had become enamored with "crystal power." She had purchased a crystal. "I was convinced it had power," she said. Little did she realize that it would open her to a satanic attack.

Our Blessed Mother has given us tools to fight evil. The Rosary, together with wearing the Scapular of Our Blessed Mother are our chief weapons. Holy Water is also recommended by the Church.

MEDJUGORJE

I have shared with you that my visit to Medjugorje, Yugoslavia was a turning point in my own life, as well as that of our community. The vast majority of priests who went there came back changed men....and Marian priests. In addition to our own conversion experience, we have seen lives changed through the power of the Sacrament of Penance. Perhaps the greatest miracles worked through the intercession of Our Lady have been in this great sacrament. Priests have also found their love for Jesus in the Eucharist is renewed and refreshed.(10)

The chief messages given by Our Lady, prayer, fasting, Love of the Eucharist and the power of the Holy Spirit are all found in the New Testament. You cannot come away from Medjugorje without a greater love for Our Blessed Mother, who invariably leads you to Jesus.

On my third trip to Medjugorje, I had the great privilege of having a cup of tea with Marija Pavlovic, one of the visionaries. We had brought a large group of young people with us to Yugoslavia, but I was able to slip away from the group for a short period of time. Marija invited me into her home and offered me this refreshment. It was just one more gift Our Lady gave to me. "Marija," I asked, "how would you summarize the message Our Lady is giving us here in Medjugorje?" The young woman stood up, raised her right hand to the sky and shouted, "Repent."

Our Blessed Mother had given this message in Medjugorje: "Tell all my sons and daughters, tell the world and as soon as you can, that I wish for their conversion. I shall pray that God may not put you to the test. You do not know, you cannot know or imagine what God is about to send upon the world if you do not convert."

In early 1992, Marija came to the United States to see her doctor. At an earlier date, she had donated one of her kidneys to her brother. The operation had been done in this country.

This visit gave Marija the opportunity to speak to a group of Marian priests in Baton Rouge. Marija spoke of the war that was raging in much of Yugoslavia. Despite this turmoil, the little town of Medjugorje has been untouched. It's almost as if the war itself is a parable. Medjugorje is an example of the Remnant Church. Despite their problems, the remnant is spared the destruction that other areas of Yugoslavia have suffered.

Many of the priests in Baton Rouge were shaken by the severity of the war in Yugoslavia. Marija warned the priests who were on this retreat that the very same thing could happen here in the United States. "In the beginning, the people in Medjugorje did everything that Our Lady asked. They prayed, fasted, and went to Church every night," Marija said. "Once the huge influx of visitors started to visit, greed set in. Many families built new homes to accommodate the pilgrims.

Profit replaced prayer in the lives of many," Marija explained.

The lesson should not be lost to any of us. Marija encouraged us that prayer and sacrifices could lessen the coming trials but it would not do away with them completely. Have we been living the messages of Mary? Do we fast on Wednesday and Friday? Do we say the complete fifteen decades every day? Do we read the Scriptures daily? The sad fact is that many of us who have been touched by Our Lady in Medjugorje are yet to be totally converted.

Our Blessed Mother is giving the children ten secrets in Medjugorje. The ninth and tenth secrets are quite serious. They contain chastisements for the world. Punishment is inevitable. Prayer and penance will lessen the severity.

Marija was given an added warning. This is the century of Satan. His power will be destroyed. The Evil one is responsible for destroying marriages and creating divisions among priests. "You must protect yourself," Our Lady said, "by prayer and fasting. Carry blessed objects with you, put them in your home and restore the use of holy water." This is one of the reasons all of the children at St. Margaret Mary are given scapulars of Our Blessed Mother to help protect them from Satan. They are enrolled in the Brown scapular.

[1]Alphonse Cappa, S.S.P., *Fatima Cove of Wonders* (Boston, MA: Daughters of St. Paul), 48.

[2]Ibid.

[3]*Queen of Peace Newspaper, Special Edition II*,

Pittsburgh Center For Peace, 6111 Steubenville Pike, McKees, Rocks, Pa. 15136.

[4]Alphonse Cappa, S.S.P., *Fatima Cove of Wonders* (Boston, MA: Daughters of St. Paul).

[5]Martin Malachi, *The Keys of This Blood* (New York: Simon & Schuster, 1991).

[6]*Queen of Peace Newspaper, Special Edition II*, Pittsburgh Center For Peace, 6111 Steubenville Pike, McKees, Rocks, Pa. 15136.

[7]Yasud Teiji, O.F.Mm (John Haffert, English version), *The Tears and Message of Mary* (Ashbury, N.J.: 101 Foundation, 1989).

[8]R. Vincent, *Please Come Back To Me And My Son: Our Lady's Appeal Through Christina Gallagher* (Westmeath, N. Ireland: Ireland's Eye Publications, 1992).

[9]Ibid.

[10]Rev. Msgr. Richard L. Carroll, V.F., *A Priest looks at Medjugorje* (New York: Vantage Press, 1989).

Chapter 14
THE KEYS TO THE TRIUMPH OF THE IMMACULATE HEART

I believe that each one of you reading this book wants to be part of the TRIUMPH OF THE IMMACULATE HEART OF MARY Our community at St. Margaret Mary has been led to see certain keys that are necessary for us to be part of this great event. There are probably others that you have learned through the Holy Spirit. Each of us has part of the puzzle. When it all comes together, we will be A Remnant Church. THE TRIUMPH OF THE IMMACULATE HEART WILL OCCUR.

KNOW THE ENEMY - IT IS SATAN HIMSELF

St. Paul warned us that our battle will be against "Powers and Principalities" i.e., Satan and his legions. If you know that the enemy is Satan, then you will use the appropriate weapons that the Church recommends to us.

Our Lady told Christina Gallagher about the tremendous power of the Rosary. "Our Lady said to me, 'tell people to arm themselves with the Rosary and never let it be out of their hearts. It will protect them during the times of TRIALS AND SUFFERINGS.'" Mary is speaking of fifteen decades, the entire Rosary, not just five decades each day.

SUPPORT THE HOLY FATHER

We have already seen that Pope John Paul II is very special to Our Blessed Mother. It is important that we have absolute loyalty to the Pope.

With the publication of the Universal

Catechism, you will find shrill voices criticizing the Pope. We have already heard a chorus of voices raised in protest about one doctrine or other with which individuals disagree.

In the final analysis, this means that we cannot pick and choose which doctrines or beliefs we will or will not accept. Christina Gallagher received an important message from Jesus on September 21, 1990. *"The three sins which grieve My heart most are abortion, the killing of the innocents, and the immoral abuse of the innocents."*

In the story of Our Lady of Guadalupe, it struck me deeply how prior to their conversion the Aztecs in Mexico were sacrificing their children to pagan gods. Through the miracle of Our Lady of Guadalupe, the mass conversion of the Indians stopped the needless slaughter of children. Perhaps the abortion crisis, the killing of more than one and a half million innocents each year in this country will be stopped through the powerful intercession of Our Blessed Mother.

We must accept the teaching of the Pope if we are to be loyal to him. For committed Catholics, we must learn to obey regardless of what the rest of the world teaches.

WE HAVE NOTHING TO FEAR

The power of our witness would be seriously affected if we are perceived as fearful people.

This is a cardinal principal. We must not focus on the trials, but look to the TRIUMPH OF THE IMMACULATE HEART OF MARY. We should long for the coming era of peace.

This freedom from fear is confirmed by Christina Gallagher. She was given an awesome vision on December 20, 1991. She saw the world plunged into the depths of sin and was told we would drink of its bitterness. "The clock is set, its alarm is set. The hour is close. Pray, Pray, Pray," Christina was told.

Our Blessed Mother had told Christina, "My child, the Purification will come. THOSE WHO HAVE SERVED GOD IN HIS LIGHT NEED NOT FEAR".

PRAY FOR THE VICTIM SOULS IN YOUR COMMUNITY

In every parish there are victim souls like Katie Hernandez and Ted Besh. Suffering is a mystery. It was through Katie that I learned a little of the meaning of surrender. I have learned a little of the importance of the virtue of patience from Ted. Too often, as people get old, they are given the opportunities of being victim souls and squander that chance. Many fail to use these opportunities of being victim souls by joining their sufferings to that of Jesus Christ.

Recently there was a description of a terminally ill patient in the daily paper whose life was ended by Dr. Kervorkian. The value of suffering is not understood in our world. Certainly many can be brought back to Divine grace through their own suffering. The millions of AIDS patients worldwide can become victim souls - for themselves and others.

Christina Gallagher was given a vision to explain the value of victim souls. Christina described it this way: "As I was given this, it was as if there were two hands, the paralyzed hand and the working hand. The paralyzed hand represents the person that cannot be bothered about God without God's grace and the other hand, the soul that will really suffer and pray harder to convert that other soul. The working hand has to do twice as much work in order to compensate for the paralyzed hand. What Jesus wants to do is to flow His grace of conversion from the working hand to the paralyzed hand and in this way through someone else's suffering. He renews His life in that soul and that is called conversion".

"...What we have to realize is that it is through the Cross that we come closer to Christ. Those who respond through surrendering to God in all things are brought closer to Him, but also, the more He will give us in trials and suffering."

"...I was made to realize that those who respond and surrender to God are the ones He wants to draw into His seven degrees of grace. I saw seven steps, and the more we respond, God raises that soul to a higher degree of His grace. By surrendering to the Cross for the love of Christ, the more you are drawn into the degrees of His grace."

PLEAD FOR DIVINE MERCY

One of the things our community at St. Margaret Mary does prior to the evening Mass is recite the Chaplet of Divine Mercy after the recitation of the rosary.

In God's eyes, each one of us is a sinner. There is not one among us who does not need Divine Mercy. We will discuss Divine Mercy in greater detail in a later chapter.

It is in the Sacrament of Penance that most of us experience the gift of Divine Mercy. It is Jesus

Christ who forgives my sins and yours in this wonderful sacrament. The opportunity to have our sins forgiven in Penance is a manifestation of Divine Mercy.

PRAY FOR PRIESTS

Our Blessed Mother has frequently asked that you pray for priests. It is clear that Satan has targeted the clergy and religious.

Christina Gallagher shared a beautiful and encouraging word about the clergy. Mary said: "We must always pray for priests, they are so very special - the bridge between God and man. God has given them the power to forgive our sins in confession and even God obeys His priests, as through the power of the Holy Spirit. They turn bread and wine into the Body and Blood of Jesus at the consecration in every Mass. They will be attacked more than lay people because they are the ones who are over His flock and have such an influence on believers. We must pray that they will be surrounded by the Light of God and protected because they are so valuable to us."

I have often been asked what should a parishioner do if her pastor is opposed to Marian devotions? Our Lady gives us an answer through Christina. Mary said: "God is depending on your prayers and mine for his priests so that they can be enlightened in the Truth. As long as we pray for them, and make sacrifice and fast, He will enlighten them."

PRAY, PRAY, PRAY

The ark of the Church will survive in your community only if it is a house of prayer. If belief in the Real Presence of Jesus is in a community, the Eucharist takes on the character of Prayer. The Mass becomes boring only if we fail to believe in the "true presence" of Christ in Holy Communion.

Our children are learning to pray in school. The fifty minutes a week that each class spends in a cenacle of prayer is a powerful tool for developing a relationship with Jesus and His Mother, Mary. I was thrilled to hear a proud father tell me how his seven year old son asked that he bring him to the prayer garden on Saturday so that he could pray.

When we pray, we must pray with our heart. This means that we must forgive anyone who has hurt us. Forgiveness is a key element to praying the way Our Lady asks.

If we pray this way, it will call us to repentance. When Our Lady asks that we go to confession once a month as she has asked at Medjugorje, we must listen. Many priests have damaged their own spiritual lives by failing to listen to Our Mother.

I praise God for the women in our community. They are the experts in prayer. This is why I am so pleased that so many of them have volunteered to teach the children to pray.

One of the Franciscan priests in Medjugorje told this story about Marija. In one message, Marija was told by Our Lady only, "PRAY PRAY PRAY! " Marija was heartbroken until her confessor told her how important this message is for each of us. We just need to put it into practice.

Christina Gallagher was told by Our Lady the importance of prayer. "...I desire my chosen children of Light to be united in me in prayer from your heart...Through you, my little one, I desire great work for the salvation of the world. You, little ones of the Lamb, will be triumphant in My Immaculate Heart. Many of my little ones are being lost."

Our Lady then asked Christina to spread her message about her "LITTLE HOUSE OF PRAYER." "I desire to gather my children together. You, my child, pray the rosary with my children as I have taught you. I entrust you with this. Do not be afraid. There is no place for fear. I will be present in this house with many angels praying with all my children."

Although this request of Christina seems to be for a specific place of prayer in Ireland, I believe that every Remnant Church **must become a little house of prayer. Russia will be converted and peace will come. ... but first we must Pray, Pray, Pray.**

St. Dominic, in the thirteen century, predicted that the Church would one day be saved by those who pray the rosary and wear the scapular of Our Blessed Mother.

EUCHARISTIC PRAYER

In Medjugorje, the children were told: "The Mass is the most excellent form of prayer." The first thing that usually happens to someone who has a religious conversion is that Mass is no longer perceived as boring. Instead of going to church only on Sunday, they will attend daily Mass if at all possible.

Your parish church or chapel can become a powerhouse of prayer, but for that to occur you must teach clearly the doctrine of the Eucharist. Bishop William K. Weigand of Salt Lake City, writing in the *Intermountain Catholic,* the diocesan newspaper, calls the Eucharist the "most central teaching of our Catholic faith." He said, "Whole generations of Catholics have been raised with imprecise language and a vague understanding of it."

Bishop Weigand went on to write that most Catholics do not understand that when they receive the Eucharist, they "are really and truly RECEIVING THE BODY, BLOOD, SOUL AND DIVINITY OF THE LORD Jesus Christ."

The Bishop told Utah Catholics to stop referring to Holy Communion as the "bread" and the "wine." It is "THE BODY OF CHRIST, THE BLOOD OF CHRIST."

Bishop Weigand cites several reasons for the lack of understanding on the part of Catholics. The Bishop suggests the following may be some of the reasons that may have contributed to the erosion of respect for the Eucharist: the change from Latin to the Vernacular in the Mass, the reception of Holy Communion in the hand, standing rather than kneeling for Holy Communion, and **a failure to visit church to pray before the Blessed Sacrament**. Unfortunately, many of our churches stay locked up most of the day. Sadly, many of our Catholics receive Holy Communion when they know or should know they are in mortal sin.

Knowledge about Jesus is not enough. We must come to love Him and this is what **Perpetual Adoration of the Blessed Sacrament accomplishes.** When more than 500 parishioners spend at least an hour a week in prayer before the Blessed Sacrament, your church becomes **A House Of**

Prayer.

You will recall the beautiful vision of St. John Bosco. In his vision, the Saint saw the Church as a ship being tossed by rough waves. The captain looks much like our present Pope as he steers the ship. Two columns of light guide him, one is Our Blessed Mother, the other is the Holy Eucharist in a monstrance that is used for adoration.

Of all the things that we can do to develop a Remnant Church, **it seems to me that Perpetual Adoration of the Blessed Sacrament and Devotion of Our Blessed Mother are most essential. The triumph of the Immaculate Heart of Mary will come aided by those who love Mary and love Jesus present both at Mass and in the Tabernacles of our Catholic Churches.**

FATHER MOSSY GALLAGHER

On January 23, 1982, St. Margaret Mary welcomed Father Mossy Gallagher as an associate pastor. Father Gallagher is a member of the St. Patrick's Fathers, a missionary order from Ireland. Father Gallagher served in Africa before coming to the United States. His stay with us was interrupted for another short tour of mission work in Africa before returning to resume his ministry in our midst in July, 1991.

Father Gallagher is noted for his devotion to the sick in the hospital, nursing homes, and shut-ins. However, he is an inspiration to all of us for his daily hour before the Blessed Sacrament. Father Gallagher shares his testimony with us:

As I reflect on my life now, I see more clearly the people who influenced me in a very significant way. My mother instilled into us, her family, reverence and devotion to the Blessed Sacrament. Since she was a teacher, I experienced that influence both at home and at school.

As I moved into the teenage years, that teaching was reinforced by the example of a young associate, Father O'Connor. I began to notice how often he was to be found praying in the presence of the Blessed Sacrament. Later on, at nineteen, when I entered the seminary, I met another priest, Father Plunkett who was so obviously a man of prayer, most of which he offered in front of the Blessed Sacrament.

There was something about these priests that attracted me and inspired me to try to be like them. They were very ordinary men, very human with a sense of humor that enabled them to take life seriously, but not themselves. They were so obviously like the rest of men and yet they had some kind of power that drew me and others to them.

As I came closer to my ordination and had read and studied more scripture, I was convinced that I had found the source of their power. I read The Gospel of Luke Chapter 8, and came upon the account of the woman who was healed by Jesus just by touching the hem of His garment.

In spite of the crowd that surrounded Him, Jesus asked, "Who touched me?" "Somebody touched me; I know that power has gone forth from me." (The Gospel of Luke 8:46) These words of Jesus have been the source of energy for me during 44 years in the priesthood.

I became more aware of this as we began Perpetual Adoration here at St. Margaret Mary in 1983, and I felt drawn to spend one hour a day in the chapel. Like the woman in the Gospel, I had many ailments of body and spirit. There were times when my "motivational" battery needed to be recharged, when I felt more than the usual warfare of Satan wearing me down. At other times, I would feel a cloud of depression moving into my life, or I would feel anger or fear getting a hold on me.

Whatever it was that was dragging me down, I would still remain faithful to the Holy Hour. It might be a struggle to stay for the full hour, but the more I struggled, the more I felt the need of staying close to Jesus. I would tell Him that I was His patient, coming for radiation treatment. Some days, all I would do was just sit in His presence, absorbing His healing rays.

He has never failed me and knowing my weakness, He would never leave me to wait for too long. I don't remember any of those periods of dryness lasting for more than a week. Then I would return to a "high" that would make the week of trials and dryness seem like a small price to pay.

I would never start an hour without inviting Mary to join with me. I would say to her; "I know for sure that Jesus your Son is here, and wherever He is, you are not far away. Help me during this hour and if my mind wanders, or I even fall asleep," as often happened, "you take over."

****

EVANGELIZE

In his letter, St. James gives us the reason we should evangelize. "Remember this: the person who brings a sinner back from his way will save his soul from death and cancel a multitude of sins." (James 5:20) Since the beginning of the

R.C.I.A. process for converts, we have seen a major change in bringing people to Jesus Christ.

This process works because it involves sharing our own faith stories. Each large group is subdivided into a smaller one. Each person, weekly, has the chance to share what Jesus is doing in their lives. As the priest presenter, I too am called upon to share my journey in faith. I am ably assisted by two deacons, Clarence Vicroy and John Weber. The sharing groups are led by 12 leaders.

Our evangelization effort is soon to take another step forward. As part of the 200th anniversary of the Archdiocese of New Orleans, we will be involved in a campaign to raise funds for the inner city schools, as well as money for the major seminary and retirement for priests.

This will give us the opportunity to call on every family in the parish. I plan to distribute a free copy of this book to each family. I believe we are a Remnant Church. I want to share with each family the wonderful things the Holy Spirit has done in this parish.

There is also a sadness I experience as I realize that many have left the Church founded by Jesus Christ. Perhaps it was the faults or failings of me or another priest that have driven them from their Father's arms. If so, this will be another opportunity to welcome home our sisters and brothers.

I believe that we are living in the times predicted in the Book of Revelation. I want each member in our church family to feel a sense of pride in what the Holy Spirit has done in our family. I also want them to feel a sense of forgiveness; asking pardon from Jesus and giving it to those who may have hurt, or injured them.

LOOK FORWARD TO THE COMING OF JESUS THROUGH THE POWER OF THE HOLY SPIRIT

I feel that many of us are experiencing the outpouring of the Holy Spirit that was requested by Pope John XXIII in 1960. We have seen dramatic events in the lives of both young and old. The phenomenon of religious experiences today is truly extraordinary.

I have been lead to pray simply that I not be a barrier to the power of the Holy Spirit in this community. I feel that often the Holy Spirit cannot work because of petty jealousy among different groups.

One of the most dramatic moments in each Sunday liturgy now is the singing of a song to the Holy Spirit just before the priest or deacon preaches. The song is "Spirit of the Living God." We ask Him first to fall afresh on him, i.e. the one who will preach. Then we pray...fall afresh on us.

One of the most powerful ways Jesus manifests himself in our presence is the gift of healing through the Holy Spirit. This is often experienced through the gift of tears.

HEALING OF LINDA JEFFERSON

On the weekend of January 23-24, 1993, Linda Jefferson, shared her experience of healing through the Holy Spirit at all the Masses except for the one for the children. As a young woman, Linda's parents went through a bitter divorce. Angry at God, Linda began to live with her boyfriend and soon became pregnant.

The experience of her first abortion was devastating. As the physician in New York turned the vacuum on, Linda tried to stop him, "It's too late," he told her. As Linda left the doctor's clinic, she vomited on her boyfriend and in his new sports car. The relationship ended and Linda moved to Florida.

Once she relocated, Linda found herself immersed in drugs, alcohol and promiscuous behavior. After a night of drinking, Linda found herself in a stranger's bed. It wasn't long after that she discovered she was pregnant, and an abortion seemed the only logical thing to do. However, complications resulted and she was forced to have a hysterectomy.

It was at this stage in her life that Linda met her husband of twelve years. Despite the grace of sacramental forgiveness in confession and a Catholic marriage, the guilt of abortion remained.

The Holy Spirit has led Linda to a contact with a very charismatic priest. He suggested a private ceremony in which only she and her husband would attend with a priest. During the Mass, she would name her two aborted children, which she did, Cecelia and Gabriel.

During the Mass, an amazing thing occured. Her husband saw a vision of a woman in white holding two children, a boy and a girl. At that moment Linda screamed out in pain. The woman, perhaps Our Blessed Mother, took the children back with her to heaven.

Linda herself experienced an amazing healing. Something went through her body from the top of her head to the tip of her toes the moment she cried out in agony. The pain of guilt was completely taken away.

Linda concluded her testimony, sharing one final gift of the Holy Spirit. During a healing service recently at St. Margaret Mary, Linda had a profound religious experience. The Holy Spirit allowed her to see that she had a third child. Her one regret was that due to the hysterectomy, she could never bear a child. Linda was shown by the Holy Spirit that a miscarriage had occured. This third child would, like her other two children, be in heaven awaiting her arrival.

It took amazing courage for Linda to share her testimony with our community. There was hardly a dry eye in the Church as she told her story. Her life tells not only the enormous gift of mercy that Jesus wants to give us; Linda is a witness to the healing power of the Holy Spirit.

For those who think God will never forgive you for the serious sins you have committed, Linda's testimony was meant for you. In God's eyes, we are all sinners, but we also know that we have Jesus as Our Savior.

THE SIGN

We have been told that Our Blessed Mother would leave a permanent sign in Medjugorje after the ten secrets are revealed. Christina Gallagher was told the following by Our Lady, "There will come a sign which everyone in the world, in an interior way, will experience and it is not very far away. Everyone will experience an inner awareness and they will know that this is from God, and they will see themselves as they really are in the sight of God. It is up to each one of us to help as many people as we can by our prayers, so that when this supernatural sign comes, they will change and will be able to respond to that sign and be saved for God." (1)

THE TRIUMPH OF THE IMMACULATE HEART OF MARY THROUGH ENTRUSTMENT

Entrustment

In a recent meeting of the deans, Archbishop Schulte used the word entrustment. He pointed out how the present Pope entrusts everything he does to Our Blessed Mother. The Archbishop went on to say that he was entrusting our entire 200 year celebration as a diocese, as well as our Capital Campaign to Our Blessed Mother.

I believe that Mary is the final piece of the puzzle. It seems that since her apparition in Fatima, there have been missing pieces. In the last twenty years, different parts of the puzzle have been revealed all over the world. Now it seems that many of the pieces are in place.

TOTAL CONSECRATION

As each of us struggle to make our communities a Remnant Church, we are trying to preserve our Catholic faith. We now realize that we are at war with Satan and we must use every tool at our disposal. I have shared with you our struggle.

I realize that the predictions at Fatima will take place. When we asked Marija, the visionary from Medjugorje, if the punishments could be eliminated, she told us they could be lessened, but not completely taken away.

On December 8, 1992, our entire community made a public ACT OF CONSECRATION TO Jesus

THROUGH Mary at every Mass. We will renew this Act of Consecration, on March 25, 1993. Those making this Total Consecration should begin their preparation on February 20.

Many of us have learned that either you become a slave to Jesus, through Mary, or a slave to the world. We have a choice of slavery, or freedom; the kingdom of heaven, or the kingdom of the earth. The two kingdoms are mutually exclusive. Put in its simplest form, we must choose between the world, the flesh and the devil and Jesus Christ as Our Lord and King.

In his own life, Jesus showed how decisively He rejected the glamour of the world. After working a miracle, the Jews wanted to make Him a worldly king - just like David. Jesus fled into the desert. When Pilate, the Roman governor, asked Jesus if He is a king, He tells him His kingdom is not of this world. In other words, it is in Heaven.

The Jewish leaders would have welcomed Jesus if He had been a worldly king. They longed for a messiah that would rid them of the yoke of Roman rule, but Jesus preached a Kingdom not of this world. The Jewish leaders at least understood what many of us fail to grasp, that you cannot have both, "Either you will be with me or against me," Jesus told His followers. Many modern day Christians preach a feel good theology. You can accommodate yourself to the values of the world and still have Heaven besides. You are told that Jesus wants everyone to be rich, or He wants everyone healed. This is not the teaching of Jesus Christ.

Jesus clearly understood the choice. If you are a slave to the world, the flesh, and the devil, you will not have the freedom to be a child of God. If you are a slave to Jesus Christ, you will be free from the influence of the world, the flesh, and the devil. The greatest slaves today are those who are addicted to sin. **The only truly free are those who are slaves of Jesus Christ.**

Like the Apostles before us, we find it difficult to understand that freedom from one involves slavery to the other, and vice versa. As the Apostles were walking to Jerusalem for the last time, they were fighting over who would have the highest place in the kingdom. They longed for power, Jesus promised them a cross. They wanted riches and He told them He didn't have a place to lay His head. They wanted the privileges of royalty and He told them if they wanted to be His disciples, they must wash each others' feet.

Jesus never gave His disciples the impression you could have the good things of the world and Heaven besides, "It is easier for a camel to enter through the eye of a needle than for a rich man to enter Heaven," Jesus warned. The eye of a needle was a very low gate in the wall of Jerusalem. It was quite difficult to get a camel through that gate.

On the crucifix you see the letters INRI. There is no "I" in Latin, so it stands for "J", Jesus Nazarenum rex Judaeorum..."Jesus" of Nazareth, King of the Jews," Pilate wrote.

Although Jesus was condemned by the Jewish Sanhedrin for claiming to be the Son of God, the Roman governor, Pilate, sentenced Him to death for maintaining that He was a king...the crime of insurrection.

Slavery or freedom, that is the choice. Through Total Consecration, we choose to be slaves of jesus through Mary. By that decision, we are free from

the slavery of the world, the flesh, and the Devil.

CONCLUSION

At times, the modern priest feels very much like St. John. Our calling is to stand under the cross with Mary, the Mother of Jesus. The pain for John must have been almost unbearable. For just one instant, I was able to taste a moment of that pain, as I watched Katie Hernandez dying. It seemed to me that watching this four year old, I saw the daily pain of her mother. There were moments I thought my heart would break.

What a struggle it must have been for St. John. Of all the apostles, he probably loved Jesus the most. The crowd was unbelievably cruel. Didn't they know this was the mother of the dying Jesus? Yet John didn't flinch, he was there for Jesus, but he was there for his Mother Mary as well.

Today there are a multitude of priests standing under that cross. The runaway apostles must have convinced themselves, "He doesn't need me. If Jesus is God, He will save Himself. If He isn't, we're all fools and have wasted our time." But, like St. John, many priests have learned that our place is under the cross near Mary.

In one of our Teams meetings, a Marian group, comprised of a priest and lay couples, Mike had a religious experience. It happened at Paul and Ellie's home. Carl, another member of our Teams, was sharing a wonderful religious experience which he had. Mike, a typical skeptical scientist, leaned over to Paul and said something, indicating he didn't believe a word of what he was hearing. All of a sudden, Mike started crying, "Excuse me for crying, but Jesus is standing behind Father Carroll with His hand on Father's shoulder and smiling". Mike said later as he elaborated to Veralyn, that Jesus was in a white robe and appeared as a real person, not a statue, image, or something.

Because Mike is basically skeptical and because he had this prior experience, I was inclined to listen more carefully to his next religious experience. On September 5, 1992, we had our regular Teams of Our Lady dinner, at Luis and Toni's home. Mike was seated in a recliner in front of a corner bookcase in their den. I was directly opposite Mike. Behind me was a corner of the den with a crucifix on a wall, surrounded by pictures of Katie Hernandez, our deceased "angel". Mike started to cry, "Excuse me for crying, but I am seeing Father Carroll on the crucifix behind where he is sitting, instead of Jesus." Mike was upset by it for the rest of the night. He later told me that the odd thing was that I was not dressed in priestly garments, but in clothing like I wore that night to our Teams meeting.

Of course, I had been thrilled to know that Jesus had His hand on my shoulder in His earlier religious experience. The vision of the cross shook me up. Father Deeter had told us some months ago in Baton Rouge that Our Lady had warned him through Father Jozo that we will experience PERSECUTION.

In an interview in October, 1981, Pope John Paul II, had grasped his rosary and said: "Here is the remedy against evil, Pray, Pray, and ask for nothing more. Leave everything else to the Mother of God." His Holiness continued: "We must be prepared to undergo trials in the not-so-distant future; trials that will require us to be ready to give up, even our lives and a total gift of self to Christ and for Christ. Through your prayers and mine, it is possible to alleviate this tribulation, but it is only in this way, that the Church can be effectively renewed. How many times indeed has the renewal of the Church been effected in blood? This time again it will not be otherwise. We must be strong. We must prepare ourselves. We must **entrust ourselves to Christ and to His Holy Mother and we must be attentive to the prayer of the Rosary."**(2)

I believe every priest today must be willing, like John, to stand under the cross. But the encouraging thing is this, the women and men of prayer will be standing by our side...and so will Our Blessed Mother!

It must have been the grace of the Holy Spirit that kept John under that cross. The same can be said of the modern day priests who have remained loyal. It's not that each of us hasn't been tempted to flee. But the apostle's words keep ringing true: "Lord to whom shall we go YOU HAVE THE WORD OF ETERNAL LIFE."

So we stayed under the cross, scarred and scared! Some of our friends thought we were fools. In the eyes of the world, we certainly aren't a success.

And then we were given the greatest grace of all. Dying on the cross, Jesus looks down and ENTRUSTED HIS MOTHER TO John. But Jesus did much more than that, He entrusted Mary to each priest for all times. Mary became OURS, but most of all, we PRIESTS BECAME HERS!

There have been times in my life and in the lives of my fellow priests that I have disappointed Our Lady. I am sure some of the tears she shed on Calvary were for me as well as my brother priests.

I have often wondered when Jesus selected His apostles why He didn't pick smarter or better men. He hasn't changed His pattern yet. Scripture tells us that He chooses the weak to confound the wise.

THE REST OF THE STORY

Each of you could write the end of the story. THE TRIUMPH OF THE IMMACULATE HEART OF MARY WILL OCCUR SOON. We will endure a period of great trials, apostasy, the rejection of the faith may overshadow the physical trials.

Russia will be converted because a network of prayer will form to protect the Church. The Holy Spirit will empower millions to find Jesus Christ and the Church will reemerge as she did on the First Pentecost.

THE WORLD WILL NOT END! A glorious period of Peace will prevail. The woman who conquered Satan will reign not only as Queen of Heaven, but now as Queen of the Earth as well.

St. John taught us an invaluable lesson. Because of his courage to stand under the cross, Our Lady was entrusted to him. We too, must be willing to stand the heat of the cross to enjoy the crown of victory.

A CALL

The Battle of Jericho should have warned us. God likes to use a REMNANT to show that the victory is due to Him and not to our power. Joshua stands for every priest in every parish throughout the world. Satan will not be defeated by a hoard but a handful.

A good friend of mine asked me months ago

why I was writing this book. At first I thought it was because I wanted to share what the Holy Spirit was doing in this community. We had a small piece of the puzzle. Perhaps if we shared it with others, we would all grow closer to the Lord.

I knew I was also writing this book for my own Catholic brothers and sisters who have left the faith. Perhaps something here may touch your heart as the Lord uses me to welcome you home. You too can be part of the Remnant Church.

I now realize that I wrote this for perhaps one brother priest who feels overburdened. I wanted to share with you what I learned, that Mary has a special love for each one of us, her priest sons, even if at times we have acted more like the prodigal one.

But most of all it was written because of a deep personal love for Mary, the Mother of Jesus who is also my mother. I wanted to put in words what I have felt in my heart the three times I visited Medjugorje. I wanted to tell her that I am so happy that I stayed under the cross. There have been times when I wanted to run, but I simply couldn't bring myself to leave Mary there alone, under the cross. I wanted to thank her for her intercession in helping our community to be selected as part of the Remnant Church.

I finally understand the meaning of ENTRUSTMENT. "Lord, I will do my best to take care of your mother," St. John must have said. He took the words out of my mouth. "I don't care how tough it gets, with your grace Lord, I'll be there for her and for Your people." Entrustment means that my mother Mary will take care of me and the entire Remnant Church, for being her slave has its reward. I have been Entrusted to Her as well!

What is the Remnant Church? We are people who have fallen hopelessly in love with a woman who had the courage to stay under the cross and watch her Son die to save us. Each of us has been rewarded by being charged to care for His Mother. Mary, the Mother of the Church has been ENTRUSTED TO OUR CARE.

But Jesus did much more for us, **he entrusted each of us to Mary, as Our Mother. It made us become like little children again, for in times of danger we flee to Her protection. Every Catholic and certainly every priest, should know we belong to Her; She is Our Mother. She will protect us.**

If I could touch the hearts of non-Catholics and non- believers it would be to tell you that you, too, have a HEAVENLY MOTHER. PRAY TO JESUS; "LORD, TEACH ME TO LOVE YOUR MOTHER." If you do, in your most frightened moment, Mary will come, but most important of all, she will bring you to Jesus.

The Remnant Church are those entrusted to Mary who look forward to the triumph of The Immaculate Heart of Mary; for they know that will result in the coming of Jesus Christ through the Holy Spirit. We pray the final words of Sacred Scripture in Revelation: 22:20-21.

"The One who gives this testimony says, 'Yes, I am coming soon!' Amen! Come Lord Jesus! The Grace of the Lord Jesus be with you all. Amen!"

You, too, can be a Remnant Church. Just look for a Woman - a Woman clothed with the Sun! Listen to her words: "DO WHATEVER HE TELLS YOU TO DO!"

SIGNS OF HER PRESENCE

The gift I pray you receive is to be a member of THE REMNANT CHURCH.

[1]R. Vincent, *Please Come Back To Me And My Son: Our Lady's Appeal Through Christina Gallagher* (Westmeath, N. Ireland: Ireland's Eye Publications, 1992).

[2]*Queen of Peace Newspaper, Special Edition II*, Pittsburgh Center For Peace, 6111 Steubenville Pike, McKees, Rocks, Pa.15136.

Chapter 15
DIVINE MERCY

One of the most powerful weapons we have in this day to fight Satan is the Divine Mercy of Jesus Christ. In our community, we have begun the devotion to Jesus under the title of Divine Mercy. A brief history of this devotion is important to understand.

Helen Kowalska was born in Poland on August 25, 1905. She attended school for only two years and began work at age 9. At age 7, she knew she wanted to be a nun and at 15, her parents refused to let her go to a convent. On August 1st of 1923, she was at a dance and while there, saw Jesus covered with wounds asking her, "For how long must I support your infidelity to me?" She fled to a church. Our Lord spoke to her saying, "go to Warsaw and enter a convent."

During Mass in Warsaw, she heard the words, "Go and see this priest. Tell him everything. He will show you what to do." The priest got her a job with a pious family, but she was refused admission to the convent.

Finally on August 1, 1925, when she was 20, she was accepted by the Sisters of Our Lady of Mercy as a postulant. On April 30, 1928, she made her first vows and five years later, her final vows. Her religious name was Sister Faustina.

On May 11, 1936, doctors found she had tuberculosis. She died on October 5, 1938, at the age of 33.

On November 30, 1980, Pope John Paul II wrote his second encyclical entitled, "Rich in Mercy."

The Mission Of Sister Faustina

Jesus appeared a number of times to give her this special message:

"To inflame the whole world with complete trust in God's infinite mercy. To bring everyone to the contemplation of the Savior's pierced heart from which flowed blood and water."

The Picture Of The Merciful Christ

On February 22, 1931, Merciful Christ appeared to Sister Faustina for the first time in Plock, Poland. Jesus' right hand was raised in blessing while the left was touching his garment at the breast where two large rays came forth, one red, the other pale. Jesus said, "Paint an image according to the pattern you see with the inscription, 'Jesus, I trust in You.' I promise that the soul that will venerate this image will not perish. I also promise victory over its enemies already here on earth, especially at the hour of death. I, myself, will defend it as my own glory. I am offering people a vessel with which they are to keep coming for graces to the fountain of mercy. That vessel is this image with the inscription, 'Jesus I trust in You.' I desire that the image be venerated first in your chapel and then throughout the world.

"The two rays denote blood and water. The pale ray stands for the water which makes souls righteous. The red ray stands for the blood which is the life of souls. These two rays issued forth from the depths of My tender mercy when My agonized heart was opened by a lance on the cross. Happy is the one who will dwell in their shelter, for the just hand of God shall not lay hold of him."

Another time Jesus said, "By means of this image, I shall grant many graces to souls. It is to be a reminder of the demands of My mercy because even the strongest faith is of no avail without works."

Trust In Divine Mercy

The Redeemer told her:

"My daughter, the fire of mercy consumes me."

"Lack of confidence breaks my heart. Even more painful for me is the lack of trust in zealous persons."

"I am all love and all mercy, and a soul that trusts in Me is happy, for I, Myself, take care of her. No sin, no matter how sordid will exhaust My mercy, for the more one draws from it the more it increases."

"I want priests to proclaim My great mercy. I want sinners to come to me without any fear whatever. Even if a soul is like a fully corrupted corpse, even if, humanly speaking, there is no further remedy, it's not like that before Me. I am more generous with sinners than with the juSt. It is for them that I came down on this earth. It is for them that I shed my Blood. Pray as much as possible for those in their agony. Obtain for them trust in my mercy."

Principal Elements of Devotion to the Divine Mercy

1. Veneration of the picture of Jesus.
2. Feast of Divine Mercy, first Sunday after Easter. "I desire," says the Lord, "that the feast of My mercy be refuge and shelter for all souls especially for poor sinners."

3. Chaplet of Divine Mercy. On September 13, 1935, Sister Faustina had a vision of an angel enforcing divine justice hurling lightening and thunder. A prayer poured out: "Father, I offer You the Body and Blood, Soul and Divinity of Your dearly beloved Son, our Lord Jesus Christ, in atonement for our sins and those of the whole world." The avenging angel disappeared.

The next day she heard, "Every time you enter the chapel, repeat immediately the prayer I taught you yesterday."

Sister Faustina was told that the Chaplet of Divine Mercy is to be said using rosary beads. It is said as follows:

Our Father, Hail Mary, Apostles' Creed - On the large beads say, "Eternal Father, I offer You the Body and Blood, Soul and Divinity, of Your Dearly Beloved Son, our Lord Jesus Christ, in atonement for our sins and those of the whole world." On the ten small beads say, "For the sake of His sorrowful passion, have mercy on us and on the whole world." In conclusion say three times, "Holy God, Holy Mighty One, Holy Immortal One, have mercy on us and on the whole world."

Our Blessed Mother appeared to Sister Faustina with this promise and warning: "Fear nothing, I gave the Savior to the world. You have to speak of His great mercy to prepare the world for His coming again."(1)

In an attempt to encourage devotion to the Divine Mercy at St. Margaret Mary Church, we have placed a picture of the Divine Mercy in our chapel. We began the recitation of the Divine Mercy Novena about two years ago.

Every night prior to the evening Mass, we recite both the Rosary and the Chaplet of Divine Mercy. These are clearly the times to call on Jesus for this gift of Divine Mercy.

Our parish has also been gifted with the services of Father Ken Harney. Ken was in the Navy for twenty years. He is also a recovering alcoholic. If it were not for the Divine Mercy, Ken would either be a drunk sailor or a dead veteran. I asked him to share a brief testimony to the Divine Mercy of Jesus Christ.

FATHER KEN HARNEY'S TESTIMONY (2)

After a 30 day silent retreat, I set out to do something good and ended up becoming a priest. It certainly wasn't that way in the beginning.

I was born and raised as a Protestant in Kentucky in a semi-rural area. Most of the young men in our community went into the military or the university after high school. If you had enough money to pay tuition, you went to college. If you didn't, you went into the military, to get your military obligation out of the way so an employer would hire you. I enlisted in the Navy and became a hospital corpsman.

During my first enlistment, I converted to Catholicism and I now consider that a special grace, but not in those days. I came to believe that I had made two big mistakes in my life. The first was becoming a Catholic and the second was enlisting in the Navy. I considered both to be of no earthly or heavenly good to me. It seemed to me that everything I wanted to do, the Church was against.

In reality, I was already becoming an

alcoholic. In those days, I would stop to pray in church and roll under the pew. It became very difficult to cover 50 yards of open ground between bars and not get picked up by the civil authorities or the military police.

My image of God in those days was a celestial being that left us to wallow around in our own stew. As far as I was concerned, for all the good He was doing, I would inform Him in my prayers that I knew half a dozen sailors that could run the world better than Him.

No one can continue to live the way I was living. Almost everything became progressively worse. There was no place left for me to go. I wanted so desperately to change but I had lost hope that I could ever change. I didn't know how. Then I came into AA to stay.

Conversion for me has always been dramatic but never sudden. I was not on the road to Damascus and knocked to the ground like St. Paul. On the contrary, I am on the road to Emmaus grumbling and chewing gravel like the disciples, complaining. I had a lot of hope in our Lord and He was nowhere to be seen. In truth, He has been there all the time.

From the very beginning, before we were born or the world was created, God knew in His mind that you and I would be born. He knew the time and our place in salvation history. Whether we realize it or not, whether we accept it or not, we are intrinsically bound to Christ. I am a Catholic Priest because of the Divine Mercy of Christ.

****

FATHER JOE BENSON'S TESTIMONY

There is no glory in the fact of being illegitimate. Nor is there joy in being handed over to an orphanage by a mother unable, or unwilling, to take care of the baby. There is no call here for sympathy - just an "in the beginning". And yet there is the desire in me to share an awe at the incredible deeds of God who has looked upon me in this lowliness. Because there is no glory nor joy in the facts of my birth and early days, there can only be rejoicing in the Mercy of God who placed me in the hands of people who, in all their strengths and weaknesses, loved me as their very own and set me forth to become, "what ever God wills", as both James and Sarah Benson would say to me often.

And in their strengths and weaknesses they shared with me the joy of being human and sometimes it's incredible pain. In a strange manner they shared also with me the faithfulness of God and the depth of the faithfulness to God required that permits Him to work.

We were a household of prayer, and this was very necessary, I would come to understand, when one was dealing with alcoholism and strong-willed people. Great were the tensions at times, and yet I can honestly say that by each Saturday afternoon, there had been a resolution in time for the weekly confessions and the Sunday Mass together. This created a deep sense in me, of the sacredness of Sundays as the Lord's Day and as a Day of Peace, but the process also allowed me to seek the Lord in tense moments. I would slowly come to appreciate the presence of the Lord in situations that seemed to change little and therefore demanded a certain patience or forbearance.

The Lord would take this to a remarkable kind

of conclusion regarding my father. One December day we met, as was our wont, on one of the city's streets. I was heading home and he was off again to place his little bet and sit in the pub to see just how bad the 'pick' was. (He was not too good economically in terms of his habit.) I saw him from across the street and as I approached him I saw the visage of death. When I got to his side I asked how he was feeling and his response confirmed to me my impression: "You know, son, just a few seconds ago I felt something come over me, but I'm all right now." I would leave him and in doing so would slowly begin to cry as I walked towards my parents home.

Four months later I was to sit at his bedside and ask him why was it that he did not want to see a doctor. He reacted strongly and yet despite this I rather firmly told him that it was perhaps due to the fact that someone would tell him what he suspected already - that he was dying. I was asked to leave the room. About an hour later I was summoned to his room. This once amateur boxer, and longshoreman looked up at me with his incredible blue eyes and said, "I'm not afraid of dying. I just don't know how to deal with what will happen to your mom and you. I love you both."

From where, I know not, but just as quickly and with an unbelievable peace I said, "Dad, we love you too much to hold you here. We love you enough to let you do."

"Well, why don't you set up the appointment with the hospital."

It was Thursday.

Saturday evening I would get a call to tell me that I was needed at my parents residence. I knew immediately he had died. For me the strange thing was that I had spent quite a few hours that day speaking to others about the death and dying process in terms of dealing with grief, even sharing some of my own feelings about the upcoming death of my father. But I was not prepared for the scene when I arrived.

My mother was not in hysterics; something for which I had prepared myself. Rather she was sitting in a chair, stunned, a little lost, but what I knew to be deeply peaceful.

"Joseph, it was incredible. Your Dad, prayed for the young boy who was dying of leukemia and said he would 'lock' up before going to bed. I just heard a thud and had said: 'Jimmy, someone has fallen.' I got no answer and so I shouted louder. Still no answer. I got up to find him on the hall floor. I cradled his head. He looked at me and asked for some water. I put a pillow below his head and got him the water. He sipped a little and looking at me said: 'Sally, you do know that I have always loved you? I'm sorry for all I've done. You know, Joseph said that this would be easy. Thank you, God.'"

Looking straight at me, with one of the more incredible smiles Sally Benson could give, she said, "and he died."

Years of care and prayer, years of just hanging in there all became part of that moment when I held my mother in my arms. A woman knew she was loved, a son knew he was listened to, and God was praised.

This story was simply shared at his funeral and many, many of his tough cronies began a process of returning to a real practice of their faith.

It was as if in praying for reconciliation with one man, one family, many families were being touched by this Divine Mercy.

****

CONFESSION - The Sacrament of Divine Mercy
Initial Letter to all Parishioners on Divine Mercy
March 11, 1994

My Dear Parishioners,

In the last few years our community at St. Margaret Mary has been called to become a remnant. We have seen the outpouring of the Holy Spirit that resulted from Perpetual Adoration. We have grown spiritually because of the great devotion we have for Our Blessed Mother. Our loyalty to the Holy Father and the Catholic Church is known far and wide.

I believe the Holy Spirit is now calling us to a more intimate relationship with Jesus Christ as Lord. The next piece of the puzzle for becoming a "Remnant Church" demands a surrender to Jesus as Lord of our lives. Many of you are already planning to make the Act of Total Consecration on March 25th. All our children in St. Margaret Mary School will make this consecration.

Whether you make the Act of Consecration or not, I feel we are being led as a community to make Jesus the Lord of our lives. To do this, we need to prepare ourselves by making a complete confession of our sins. Many of you have already answered this call at our recent mission with Father Straub. Most of you have not gone to confession for years. This must change if we are going to be used by the Holy Spirit in this coming time of chastisement.

Recently I was told by one of our parishioners

of a private audience held by our Holy Father. The best friend of this parishioner attended this audience and assisted at Mass with three Jesuit priests. The four of them learned that the Pope is regularly seeing Our Blessed Mother. At Mass the Holy Father said, not once, but eight times, "We are living in the end times." I find that statement, coming from a man who all admire, awesome.

We know from the messages of Fatima, which have been approved, that our Lady warns of the impending tribulations that can be found in scripture in the Book of Revelation. But Mary promises us that in the end, Satan will be defeated. The Immaculate Heart will triumph and world peace will be achieved.

Jesus warned us through scripture that in the end times, "false prophets will arise who will lead astray even the elect." I have seen this confusion first hand. This week I received a letter from the Archbishop of Denver informing the Church that Theresa Lopez, the alleged visionary from Denver, has failed to receive Church approval. The following is a copy of Archbishop Stafford's letter. <u>Our community will submit totally to this decision.</u>

Declaration Concerning Alleged Apparitions of the Blessed Virgin Mary at Mother Cabrini Shrine and other Places in the Archdiocese of Denver

On December 9, 1991, I appointed a commission to investigate alleged apparitions of the Blessed Virgin Mary at Mother Cabrini Shrine and other places within the Archdiocese of Denver to Theresa Antonia Lopez. On February 22, 1994, the commission completed its investigation and presented its finding to me.

As Archbishop of Denver, I have concluded that the alleged apparitions of the Blessed Virgin Mary to Theresa Antonia Lopez are devoid of any supernatural origin.

Because of my concern for the spiritual welfare of the People of God, I direct the faithful to refrain from participating in or promoting para-liturgical or liturgical services related to the alleged apparitions.

Furthermore, anyone encouraging devotion to these alleged apparitions in any way is acting contrary to my wishes as Archbishop of Denver.

It remains my constant hope that all the faithful will promote devotion to Our Blessed Lady in the many forms which have been approved by the Catholic Church.

*J. Francis Stafford
Archbishop of Denver
March 9, 1994* (3)

Satan has been able to deceive me and countless others about the authenticity of Theresa Lopez and other visionaries who have failed to get Church approval. Satan is real and his power is now reaching its climax.

One way Satan has deceived countless Catholics has been in the area of the need for confession. Many of you, I know, have not gone to confession because you were told by one priest or the other that "very few Catholics commit mortal sin." This is a delusion that has affected even many priests.

There are countless Catholics who regularly miss Sunday Mass, which is objectively a mortal sin, and routinely return the following Sunday to receive communion without going to confession. This is a sacrilege and a grave sin. St. Paul warns us, "... whoever eats the bread or drinks the cup of the Lord unworthily sins against the body and blood of the Lord." I Corinthians 11:27

I believe that St. Margaret Mary parish is being led to spiritual intimacy with Jesus Christ as Lord. But now it's up to you. If you have not gone to confession for a year or more, you need prayerfully to consider doing so. We will have a Penance Service on Tuesday, March 15th at 7:30 p.m.., following the 6:30 p.m.. Mass. We will have at least six or seven priests available for confession. You need to come.

On November 13, 1980, our Holy Father, Pope John Paul II wrote an encyclical entitled, "On the Mercy of God." In this letter the Pope said:

The church lives an authentic life when she professes and proclaims mercy. The most stupendous attribute of the Creator and of the Redeemer - and when she brings people close to the sources of the Savior's mercy, of which she is the trustee and dispenser. Of great significance in this area is constant meditation on the word of God and above all conscious and mature participation in the Eucharist and in the Sacrament of Penance or Reconciliation. It is the sacrament of penance or reconciliation that prepares the way for each individual even those weighed down with great faults. In this sacrament each person can experience mercy in a unique way. That is the love which is more powerful than sin."

I believe we are now in the period of Divine Mercy. If you have been away from the Catholic Church for any reason, this is an invitation from Jesus Himself to come home. If you have been deceived as many others have by Satan, you need to understand that Satan's power has never been greater. Monthly confession should not be a luxury for the few, but a habit for the majority. You need to come Tuesday night.

We now know that Satan's favorite target has been priests. Sister Briege McKenna, the nun who prior to her call by Our Lady to a healing ministry to priests, was told that priests are Satan's favorite target. I show the scars of my failures to defeat Satan in my life. But I also know that the youth are Satan's next favorite target. My special plea is for all young people to come and hear about God's mercy.

When I made the decision that all the priests would speak this weekend on Divine Mercy, I hoped that scripture would provide us a suitable text. The second reading is from St. Paul's letter to the Ephesians, "God is rich in mercy; because of his great love for us he brought us to life with Christ when we were dead in sin. By this favor you were saved. I repeat it is owing to His favor that salvation is yours through faith. This is not your own doing, it is God's gift."

Finally, one of the things that I believe will occur during the time of chastisement is this; We will see ourselves as we really are in God's eyes. Father Joe shared a story with me. As a young priest he was called upon at an international conference of priests to hear the confession of the clergy. An elderly priest came in and demanded to know by what right this youngster had to hear his confession. "You can stay or you can leave," Joe responded. For the next hour and a half this priest poured out his sins. He had not been to confession in more than fifty years. So moved was this elderly priest that he sent a card of thanks to Joe. Six months later he died. If Satan can deceive even the priests like this, how much more easily will he deceive the laity.

At the same international conference, Leanne Payne, a pastoral counselor told the priests, "My prayer for you is that you recognize yourselves as you truly are before the Lord." Father Joe and others actually witnessed priests jump in shock at what they were experiencing.

My prayer for you, my dearest children, is to keep you under the protective custody of Our Lady. Two different individuals have seen a vision of our community under the protective bubble of Our Lady during the coming time of chastisement. But make no mistake about it, regular confession is a necessary component to secure our place in the Remnant Church.

If our Divine Savior issues you a call to repentance, I beg you to come Tuesday night, March 15th. You will never regret heeding that summons.

With deepest love,
Father Carroll

WEEKEND SERMON
March 11-12, 1994

My Dear Children,

One day when you are asked by your grandchildren to tell them a story, gather them close around the fire and tell them the story about the Ark. It wasn't Noah's Ark; it was the Ark that saved us, the church we called the Remnant. The Holy Spirit used the Virgin Mother of God to crush the serpent's head. The Church even called Mary, The Ark of the Covenant.

His name was Father Richard Carroll, the pastor of St. Margaret Mary Church in Slidell, Louisiana. On March 11, 1994 at 11:00 p.m. he returned from blessing the home of one of his precious daughters who was being subjected to the attack of Satan. She was so fearful of Satan she couldn't sleep in her room. Many people at the time didn't believe in the devil. But Our Blessed Mother knew better.

At 2:15 a.m. Saturday morning, March 12, 1994, he finished his third Rosary and listened to a wonderful tape by Kathleen Keefe from Yonkers, New York. Kathleen was a mother of seven who had a healing ministry to priests.

Although he had already prepared his homily for Saturday night Our Blessed Mother wouldn't let him sleep. Finally, he gave in and decided to write the final chapter of <u>The Remnant Church</u>.

His parishioners had heard over and over how the Holy Spirit was building a Remnant. Jesus wanted every Catholic parish to be a Remnant. Jesus had warned in scripture, "When the Son of Man comes, will He find any faith whatsoever?" Fr. Carroll was afraid that Christ would find little faith and few remnants.

Building the Ark was the easy part. More than ten years earlier our community had begun Perpetual Adoration of the Blessed Sacrament. Hundreds of parishioners spent an hour a week in adoration of Jesus. The love of Jesus in the Eucharist was phenomenal.

The Holy Spirit showed us the importance of the love of Our Blessed Mother. She confirmed that importance to us through many signs.

A few months earlier someone came in to tell him how Mary brought her into the Ark - The Remnant Church. Her baby had died inside her womb. The doctor was going to remove it surgically but first he took an ultrasound. The Protestant, whose name was Dianne, had never prayed to Mary. After all, she was a Protestant. "I don't know why I did it,"Dianne said, "but as they were taking the picture, I prayed, Mary, save my baby." At that moment, miraculously, the baby turned over in her womb and began sucking her thumb. She was born a healthy child they called Bridget.

But over seven years went by and Dianne never became a Catholic. Last year her Catholic husband convinced Dianne to attend a Charismatic conference in New Orleans. At noon, when others left for lunch they moved close to the front of the hall.

Suddenly a stranger stood before them. "Our Lady wants your daughter to pray before the Tilma," she said. The Tilma was a picture or image of Our Lady of Guadalupe, who is sometimes called Our Lady of the Americas. Bridget and her dad obediently got up to pray before the picture of Our Lady.

The stranger said to Dianne, "You asked God for a sign, if you should become Catholic." Jesus said to tell you, "when you prayed to my Mother, she came and asked me to save your child. The sign you wanted is your healthy child, Bridget." And that Protestant convert and her family were given a ticket to the Ark.

"Wait," the children listening to your story will cry! "What tickets?"

"I will tell you later," the storyteller continued.

Father Carroll learned that to be a Remnant Church, his community had to love the Pope and listen to his authority. That was easy at St. Margaret Mary because they loved Pope John Paul II.

But the old priest reminded his parishioners that it also meant obedience to the authority of the Catholic Bishops who are in union with the Pope. Father Carroll was taught that lesson by Our Lady. He had met Theresa Lopez, a reputed visionary from Denver. Theresa told of seeing Our Lady and had wonderful messages, she said were from the Mother of God. In fact, she even told Father Carroll that Mary spoke often of the Remnant Flock. Father Carroll included her story in the first edition of <u>The Remnant Church</u>.

But in early March, 1994, the Archbishop of Denver, Thomas Stafford notified the country that he had decided Theresa did not have supernatural apparitions.

Father Carroll knew what he had to do. "I have always said I will support the decision of the Church. I will not mention Theresa again. Her story will be removed from our parish book, <u>The Remnant Church</u>." Loyalty to the Holy Father means obedience to his Bishops who are in union with the Pope. At the time Our Lady said that confusion was all around. False apparitions abounded. Apparently deception isn't new. According to Michael Brown, the author of <u>The Prayer Warrior</u>, a seventeenth century mystic confused the local church for more than 30 years before it was discovered she had been deceived.

Our Blessed Mother was telling priests to bring their people back to the sacraments, particularly the Eucharist and Confession. If you do this, she promised, the outpouring of Divine Mercy would occur in our Church. Many will get a ticket to the

Ark because of this great grace.

The children hearing this story will get restless. "Tell us about the Chastisement."

"Ok," the storyteller went on. Father Carroll now knew that the Ark was nearly finished. But the surprise was how few there were to take the boat. Everyone had an excuse - after all it was exam week.

In late February, 1994, even TV had a two hour story on ancient prophets. It said much of what Our Lady was warning us all over the world. But the graphic map of the United States after the storm was a shock.

A prophet had seen a vision of storms, tornadoes and earthquakes. California had dropped into the Pacific Ocean and the East coast was vastly trimmed. Louisiana was seen to be flooded by the gulf. Denver and the Rockies were shown as the West coast of the Pacific.

The Last Piece Of The Puzzle

The Holy Spirit then gave Father Carroll the final piece of the puzzle. To prepare for the return of Jesus Christ through His Divine Mercy, our community needed to do certain things:

1. *Get the people to go to confession on March 15, 1994.*
2. *Prepare to make the Total Consecration to the Sacred Heart through the Immaculate Heart of Mary on March 25, 1994.*
3. *Plan to do the Novena of Divine Mercy from Good Friday to the Sunday after Easter, which is Mercy Sunday. For two years we had celebrated Mercy Sunday. After every*

daily Mass during the nine dayperiod, the prayer warriors said the Divine Mercy Novena of Sister Faustina.

But how could Father Carroll get them to go to confession, particularly on a school night, March 15th? That is where the tickets to the Ark came in.

"This is what you are to say to my children," Our Lady said. "On the fourth Sunday of Lent, called Rejoice Sunday, you are to announce the Good News. Each of you is invited to board the Ark. It is now finished. The time is short. Today is the Day of Grace. The Holy Spirit is inviting you to get on the Ark. Bring your children if you want to survive the coming tribulation."

But this was the problem. You have to come with your husband or wife, and your children, but you cannot take anything with you but the clothes on your back. You must trust totally in the Sacred Heart of Jesus and his Mercy. You must believe in the scriptures of Revelation 12 that Mary, the Mother of God will be used to crush the head of the serpent. You see, the Ark is not only a boat - it is Mary who is called by the Holy Mother, the Church - the one who will invite you to board the ship and leave all else behind. This is what is meant by total surrender. As Pope John Paul II says in his motto "Totus Tuus," you must belong totally to Jesus.

Father Carroll knew what that meant. Many of his children would not sense the coming trials. Some were too busy, after all everyone wants a good grade on a test. Everyone had something they were afraid to leave behind. But most were afraid to leave their sins behind.

No Room - Even For Sin

"I'm sorry," Our Lady told him. "There is no room even for the sins. The only way they can board the ship is, give up every little sin."

"On Tuesday, March 15, 1994 the Ark will depart. Only those with a ticket will be allowed to board the Ark. But the price of a ticket is total surrender," she said.

"How can I teach them in only two talks?," the old priest inquired. "In fact most of them won't even accept the invitation."

"Don't tell them," Our Lady said, "show them!" Don't preach surrender, live it and show them how."

Experiencing Divine Mercy

"Many of my priest sons seem never to have experienced Divine Mercy. Therefore, they can't explain it. You, my son have. Tell them what I did for you. If you do that, I promise, many will follow you in the boat Tuesday night. Otherwise, the Remnant will be very small. You have only 6,500 seats plus room for the children. Anyone who doesn't have a ticket will be left behind. And someone else will take their place."

He knew Our Lady meant what she said. On Friday evening at 2:45 p.m. she told him to order the tickets. "There is no one who loves Jesus enough to rush such an order," he said, "except Dudley." "But he doesn't believe in praying to Mary." "I will send him a sign," Our Blessed Mother responded.

An hour later Dudley arrived with the tickets and the sign came in the door at the same time. A very devout Lutheran came to get a Rosary blessed.

"For three nights in a row," she said, "a woman appeared to me in a dream and told me to say the Rosary."

"Was she pretty," the secretary asked?

"I couldn't make out her face, it was shaded," responded the Lutheran. "The only thing I could make out clearly was her brown hair that fell over one shoulder. I wanted to put the Rosary around my neck."

"No," the woman in the dream said, "you need to pray it."

"I don't know how," the Lutheran responded.

"Ask a friend," the woman responded, "she will tell you."

The next day her friend gave her a Rosary and a pamphlet that explained it. Get it blessed at St. Margaret Mary Church she was told.

"I am very devout. I pray every day. Now when I wake up, every morning the Rosary is on my mind. I have to learn how to say it."

The Lutheran woman's name is Mary. Father Joe Benson blessed her Rosary. Father Benson told her that Martin Luther had a great devotion to Our Lady even though modern day Lutherans do not. In fact, the symbol that Luther borrowed from the Augustinian order is found today in every Lutheran Church - it is the Sacred Heart.

The "woman" that the Lutheran saw was the same "woman" whom scripture says in Revelation 12:1, will be "... clothed with the sun, with the moon under her feet, and on her head a crown of twelve stars." It was the Blessed Mother.

"Yes," Our Blessed Mother said, *"She will get one of the tickets."*

"I hope Dudley and his wife do too," he said. *"They love Jesus so much."*

"They got an invitation," our Lady replied.

Invitation

Our Lady gave the old priest his one chance to convince his children to follow him on the boat. Father Carroll would speak at the 6:00 p.m. and 7:00 p.m. Masses; Father Joe Benson would invite some of the remnant aboard at 8:30 a.m. and 11:30 a.m. Masses. Father Mossy Gallagher will issue the call at the 10:00 a.m. Mass. Father Carroll's sermon began like this:

My Dearest Children,

The Holy Spirit has spent over ten years building up this Remnant Church through Perpetual Adoration, love of Mary and loyalty to the Pope. The Ark is now finished.

Every grace that you will need to survive the coming trials will be given you on Tuesday night, March 15th. at 7:00 p.m. at a Penance Service.

When you entered church tonight you were given a ticket to board the Ark. You have until after communion to decide if you will accept it. If you choose to reject it, your ticket will be given to another. There is room for only 6,500 plus children. But we will leave late Tuesday night. You can bring nothing with you except your children and the clothes on your back. This is what is meant by total surrender to Jesus through Mary.

But you must be willing to pay the price to trust, not me but Jesus - totally. Renounce every sin you harbor. Cut through all the lies. On Tuesday night those who accept the invitation will be given an extraordinary grace, the grace to see yourself as you really are. I told you of Father Benson's story in a recent letter, how when this prayer was prayed over a group of priests they were literally picked up bodily from their chairs. Father Joe told of the priest who had not gone to confession for 52 years, but went six months before he died. Is it any surprise many of you have soiled your baptismal robes and remained mired in sin? How can I get you to hear this prayer prayed over you on Tuesday night?

Our Lady gave me the answer! Show them!

Friday afternoon Our Blessed Mother gave me the picture. During prayer I saw myself at the Last Supper. I felt the thrill and excitement of the apostles. All, but Judas, were thrilled as Jesus said the words of consecration over the bread, "This is my body". . . and then over the wine, "This is my Blood . . . do this in remembrance of me! "

I once again felt the ecstasy of my ordination. The words of Latin rang out in my ears; you are a priest according to the order of Melchizedek. The joy of belonging totally to Jesus was indescribable.

My first Mass was reverent and pious. My father, mother, and sister beamed. My brother Ralph already a priest a year, was there at my side. Tony, my sister's husband looked like a kid.

Where did it all come apart?

I was then in the Garden of Gethsemane. Tears of blood were streaming down the face of Jesus. And then Christ hit me between the eyes. "I want you to see what your sins have done," Jesus said.

I thought committing sin was just breaking a commandment, but he said, "Sin is breaking our covenant - it is breaking my heart. It was an agreement you made with God, the Father, through Me. And I must pay dearly for each breach of that love pact."

I knew that once I made the decision to teach you surrender, I would have to pray the prayer that will be said over you Tuesday night; "Holy Spirit, let me see myself as I am." Even as I thought of the pain, I winced.

It's no secret to you. I have told you, my children, countless times that I am a sinner. All of a sudden I realized I was responsible, not only for my sins, heavy as they are, but also for your sins.

Just for a moment, imagine me Monday afternoon when I will be kneeling before Father LaFranz, my spiritual director to make a general confession of my life and pray the prayer of total surrender. "Holy Spirit, let me see myself as you see me." I will be in the Garden of Gethsemane.

How can I explain to the Father that I failed to teach you to pray because I was not a man of deep prayer? Then all the sins against the Eucharist will jump up at me. Sure, you will shout, we made sacrilegious communions, but you were our spiritual Father and look at the times you rushed through the Mass.

I knew I would see the face of every child of

mine in this community for nearly 25 years who has received communion in mortal sin. There have been thousands of sacrileges.

And Jesus will simply ask, "Did you tell them the pain it is costing me?" It's not a broken law. It's a broken body that bleeds for you and me!

How often did I preach Divine Mercy? I can remember the times I heard the confessions of the parish in fifteen minutes. And the pain will grow deeper. Sin is breaking a love relationship with God our Father, Jesus our Lord and with our family.

I began to shed tears, real tears. Because I realized it wasn't Father Carroll in that Garden of Gethsemane, it was Jesus!

Mary told me to tell you the rest of the story. I received Divine Mercy through the outpouring of love in my most sinful moments, because Our Lady dragged me, often kicking and screaming to confession at least once a month. My children, I know from my own experience the healing calm of repentance. I call you to that gift Tuesday night.

The scene moved to the cross. It was Jesus hanging there. I thought he would have criticized or blamed me but he only wanted me to say - I am sorry.

I looked around and almost everyone had run away. Mary Madgelene, the sinner, Mary the wife of Clopas, John the apostle and Our Blessed Mother were the only four there. What a remnant!

I wanted to take St. John's place and be the priest who would stand by her side. I wanted to comfort Our Lady, but when I looked it was she who was comforting John. Our Lady was comforting all of us, her sinful sons - her priests.

Finally Jesus spoke the words I needed to hear. The words you need to hear. "Father forgive them for they know not what they do."

Tuesday night will be a moment of unheralded grace for this community. This may be your only chance. It is a moment of Divine Mercy.

The Holy Spirit has built the Remnant Church - The Ark. Do you have the courage to get in? I'm not asking you to do something I won't do first.

When we gather Tuesday, I will pray this one prayer. "Holy Spirit give each of us the grace to see ourselves as we are." I also will share with you the experience of total surrender to Jesus through the Sacrament of Reconciliation that I will receive on Monday afternoon from Father LaFranz.

Each of you now hold a ticket in your hand. At communion time ask the Lord if you are truly worthy to receive His Body and Blood in Holy Communion.

If you are in mortal sin - if you severed your love relationship, your covenant with God, with Jesus - don't, I plead with you, DO NOT receive Holy Communion unworthily ever again. Instead come up and get a blessing from the priest or lay minister. You will never again be able to plead ignorance before the Father.

St. Paul clearly says, "Whoever eats or drinks of the Body and Blood of Christ, eat it unto condemnation."

Ask for the grace to sign that card. Say yes as

Mary did. Say yes, I will go to confession.

So that's what the tickets were all about. "Yes," *the storyteller concluded, "many of us came that Tuesday night. We were all ashamed and scared. But Father Carroll shared the ecstasy he felt when all his sins and yours were lifted from his soul."*

Our Lady was there and many of the children saw angels. The angels were all jumping for joy.

I can still hear the words of Jesus echoing from the cross - "Father forgive them for they know not what they do."

But as I looked around the church that night, I was amazed there were so few. I later asked the old priest how he felt that night because I saw the tears in his eyes. Most of his children had built the Ark but never rode in it.

"Father, you must have been quite disappointed?" I asked.

"You must have seen my tears," he answered.

I asked the Lord Jesus about it. "Why didn't they listen?"

I heard his answer in a loud tone, "they didn't listen to me either. That's why I wanted you to call it a remnant - the few."

And then we all saw Jesus in his dying moments turn to her, "Take care of your son - take care of all Father's children - they are part of the Remnant Church, they are family."

Surrender was a small price we paid for the tickets to heaven; if only the others had listened!

****

SERMON AT ALL MASSES
April 30 - June 1, 1994

My Dear Children:

    I would like to begin by thanking each of you for your prayers during my recent illness. It has always been my practice during the last 24 and a half years as pastor of St. Margaret Mary to stand before you to report the good as well as the bad.

    On March 12th and 13th, I preached at the Saturday 6:00 p.m.. Mass and the Sunday 7:00 p.m.. Despite the fact that it was a quite lengthy talk, it was extremely well received. At the Sunday night mass 400 individuals agreed to come to our reconciliation service on March 15, and volunteered to go to the gym so that others might have a seat in the church. In all 1,200 attended the penance service on Tuesday night.

    The sermon on the 12th and 13th of March was motivated by a deep religious experience I had the week prior. I have never before experienced or known Divine Mercy in such a clear and profound way.

    I now realize that Our Blessed Mother wanted to teach me the importance of total surrender. I had asked the other two priests in the parish to pray that <u>each of you would see yourselves as you really are</u>.

    Because of the goodness of Jesus Christ I had already seen myself as I am. I saw the heart of Jesus. It then became clear to me that my sinfulness involved a <u>sense of shame</u>. In addition to my own sin, I was ashamed of many of the men who left the priesthood; men that I knew.

The faces of many priests flashed before me. As a young priest I remembered the associate who had an illegitimate child and left the priesthood. I thought of the priest I had admired. He was my elderly pastor who decided to leave the priesthood and get married at 60 years of age. And though he later changed his mind, I was so ashamed.

But it was under the cross with Mary and John that it all came clear. My sin was my shame. For I was not just ashamed of individual priests who left the priesthood, I was ashamed of Jesus Christ himself. It was of His priesthood I had been ashamed.

And then Our Blessed Mother allowed me to realize that I was also ashamed of her. I literally thought my heart would break with the pain. I couldn't stop crying.

I finally understood that sin involved breaking a covenant relationship. But it was Divine Mercy that touched my soul. I knew Jesus as my intercessor as he pleaded with the Father; "Father forgive him, for he knows not what he does."

I was so touched by Divine Mercy that I begged for one gift only. The grace that I asked for was never to run away from the cross. If there is only one priest left under the cross, dear Jesus let it be me.

On Tuesday March 15th just hours before our penance service members of my family convinced me that for my own good as well as that of my parishioners, I should check myself into Ochsner Mental Hospital.

There were some clear medical issues that demanded attention. Nine weeks on a liquid diet had adversely affected my electrolytes. Eight weeks of a nasal infection and extreme high blood pressure had contributed to my medical problems. The Psychiatrists at Ochsner hospital initially decided that I was suffering from bipolar disorder.

I spent two weeks as an in-patient at Ochsner. The last four weeks I have been an outpatient living at my sister's home in Metairie. I was officially discharged by Ochsner on Monday. During my hospital stay at Ochsner, I was able to review my religious experience with Father John Sax, the head of personnel. It was obvious that Father Sax shared his insight with Archbishop Schulte. When the Archbishop visited me, he was quick to affirm me, assuring me I could return to St. Margaret Mary as soon as I was well. This was the best medicine I could be given.

The Archbishop also encouraged me to get a second opinion from a Psychiatrist who is an expert in the field of religious experience.

WHY GET A SECOND OPINION?

I learned that there was a psychiatrist, Dr. George Hogben in Rye, New York, who specializes in religious type experiences. I spent 4 days in Rye, meeting with Dr. Hogben. Dr. Hogben wrote the following in his report: "it is not uncommon for profound spiritual experiences to be mistaken for psychosis. This syndrome, the Kundaline Syndrome, has been described. I think Father will emerge from this whole experience with a great deal of personal and spiritual growth and be a strong leader for all of us in the difficult times we face."

OCHSNER - FINAL REPORT

On Friday, April 22nd I met with Dr. Mestayer, another psychiatrist from Ochsner. He asked that I call Dr. Tom McKean on Monday which I did. On that occasion Dr. McKean indicated to me that he and Dr. Mestayer felt that the major problem I had experienced was due to the liquid diet. It was the intention of both psychiatrists to take me off all medication in the near future.

CONCLUSION
WHAT LESSONS HAVE I LEARNED?

1. Both Dr. Hogben from New York and the two psychiatrists from Ochsner recommend limiting my work-including prayer to 40 hours a week. To do otherwise is to put myself needlessly at risk.
2. I believe that Divine Mercy is extremely important for our church at this time. Incidentally the numbers of confessions in the last month have been phenomenal. This is a supernatural consequence of Divine Mercy.

When I was in Rye I visited Kathleen Keefe and her family. The Keefe's became involved in Divine Mercy in 1982 after the healing of their infant son. In thanksgiving, they dedicated their lives to the spread of Divine Mercy. Subsequently, they have been drawn into great spiritual warfare. "The loss of worldly assets is part of the warfare," Kathleen said. "But as one is stripped of the world, one comes to experience a deeper union - a profound encounter with God's mercy. Divine Mercy is embracing the cross, something we are all called to do. As God allowed our stripping, He gave us the grace to thank Him and that is what opens the floodgates of mercy - thanksgiving"

I would like to close with just one final thought. When I found myself in a mental hospital just a few hours before one of the great spiritual events in the life of this Parish it was quite scary.

I know that one of the members of my Teams of Our Lady group had seen me hanging on the cross. Was that it? I also knew that we were all trying to learn total surrender. Was this just a lesson?

I can only tell you that it has shown me how incredibly vulnerable priests are to illness as well as spiritual attacks. I have shared my vulnerability with you, with the solid hope that prayer for your Priests will always be a priority in your family.

I would like to close with a quotation from the late Padre Pio: "the cross will never oppress you; its weight might cause you to stagger but its strength will sustain you."

THE RETREAT

During my visit to Rye, New York, Kathleen Keefe invited me to a priests' retreat at San Giovanni Rotondo, Italy, July 17, 1994. Kathleen had been led by the Lord Jesus to establish a retreat for the renewal of the priesthood at San Giovanni Rotondo. The model for priestly renewal is in keeping with Padre Pio's prophesy that San Giovanni Rotondo would be one of the great centers of spiritual renewal in the world. Father Bernie Bush. S.J. would be the retreat master. The retreat would focus on prayer, inner healing as well as recognizing the strategy of Satan in the world today.

I was very reluctant to go initially. After all my experience with Divine Mercy landed me in a mental institution. However by now, my psychiatrist Dr. Mestayer was convinced that the source of my problem was a liquid diet I had been on, to try to control my weight and high blood pressure. Nearly three weeks ago Dr. Mestayer released me and took me off medication.

Although I hesitated going on the priest's retreat, I was fascinated by Padre Pio, the deceased Capuchin. Padre Pio is buried in a tomb in the church of Our Lady of Grace in San Giovanni, Italy.

I had met a woman whose next door neighbor in Diamondhead, Mississippi had been healed years before by Padre Pio. Stranded in a foreign land, told by her doctor that she would probably die, Padre Pio appeared to her in her hospital room and told her she would be cured. The next day she was completely healed. A week before I left for the retreat a parishioner told me she had been cured of cancer through the intercession of Padre Pio.

Perhaps God wants to cure me of my blindness, I thought.

When I was only 23 I became blind in one eye. This ailment together with high blood pressure had forced me out of the seminary with little more than a year of study left. During this time I became a janitor as Our Lady tried to teach me surrender. It was only through the pleading of the rector Father Bolduc and Bishop Caillout that I was allowed to return to the seminary in order to be ordained a priest. Would Padre Pio be instrumental in curing my blindness?

Only the truly blind will be able to see!

As I look back now I realize my religious experience in March began when I prayed Scripture from The Gospel of John Chapter 9:39-40, on the cure of the blind man. Christ warned us: "... 'I came into this world to divide it, to make the sightless see and the seeing blind.' ... 'But we see,' you say, and your sin remains." The grace I received in the early part of the year was to see myself as I am. Once I recognized my blindness, I could be cured. It would involve Divine Mercy.

A few days before I left for the retreat someone put a small pamphlet on my desk by Father Philip Bebie, C.P. entitled "The Warning". It was a brief story of the apparitions of our Lady at Garabandal, Spain. I was struck by the warning which will show us our sins.. Since the church has not ruled on this apparition we must await ecclesiastical approval. However this booklet opened my eyes to the possibility that Our Lady was showing me that if this does occur and you see yourself as you really are, you will experience as I did the unbelievable <u>Divine Mercy of Jesus Christ</u>.

WHO IS PADRE PIO

The priest retreat would take place from July 17-27, 1994, in the town made famous by Padre Pio.

Padre Pio was born in Pietrelcina, Southern Italy on May 25, 1887. He entered the Capuchin Friars at the age of 15. He was ordained a priest in 1910. On September 20, 1918, the five wounds of Our Lord's passion appeared on his body. His life was given over to prayer and suffering. Padre Pio spent 12 to 15 hours a day hearing confession. He lived in Divine Mercy. Padre Pio was incredibly loyal to the church. For three years he was forbidden to be seen outside the monastery. Confined to his room or saying mass in a small Marian chapel, he refused to complain. When one of the brothers tried to elicit a complaint he silenced him immediately. "The church is your mother" he said.

Padre Pio had a deep mystical union with God and burning love for the Blessed Sacrament and Our Lady.

His celebration of Holy Mass would often last three hours, in Our Lady of Grace Church where he served for the last 52 years of his life. It is located in the town of San Giovanni Rotondo, (St. John the Baptist) about 6 hours from Rome by bus.

Perhaps Padre Pio was a modern John the Baptist pointing out to the priests of our time the need to preach repentance through Divine Mercy. *I believe that Jesus Christ will come in our time through His Divine Mercy.* If sufficient numbers truly repent from their sins and receive Divine Mercy, the chastisements can be averted.

SERMON - THE RETREAT
July 28, 1994

My Dear Children:

I have just returned from the priest's retreat at the site of the tomb of Padre Pio in San Giovanni Rotondo, Italy. Enclosed in this letter is a gift. This holy card, which is a picture of Padre Pio, contains a third class relic. I ask you to cherish it as you pray for the canonization of Padre Pio, a Capuchin monk gifted with the stigmata, the five wounds of Jesus Christ.

I also want to assure you that I have placed your intentions and needs at the altar near the tomb of Padre Pio, St. Michael's cave and St Peter's tomb in Rome.

I am sure that one of the questions you will want to know, was why did I go so far to make a retreat. I believe that Our Lady called me there for a purpose.

The Spiritual Journey

I will have to retrace my steps briefly on this spiritual journey. For a brief period in March, I was gifted by Our Lady with a spiritual experience that I now feel each of you may go through. Happily it will be easier since I have walked that road already, and you will know that it is all about Divine Mercy.

During this time I was shown by Our Lady, the heart of Jesus and her own heart. Our Lady made me aware of my major sins. I learned my major sin was shame. I learned that this shame was due to my own sins. I later learned that this shame was also due to sins of past generations. Primarily my shame was due to my feelings about the priesthood. I felt ashamed as I read about pedophelia. I was ashamed about the 100,000 priests who left the ministry during the last 35 years. I felt shame!

Our Lady showed me that my shame over the priesthood resulted in my being ashamed of the priesthood of Jesus. It also meant I was ashamed of Mary, our mother. This nearly broke my heart. The retreat in Italy would heal this hurt that had already been forgiven in the Sacrament of Penance.

Most of you, my dear children know much of the story already. You were told of Our Lady's plea in March to go to confession. 1,200 of you bought a ticket on the ark. You paid for it with the blood of

Christ when you went to confession on March 15, 1994.

During this time, I was called to suffer. I spent two weeks in a mental hospital at Ochsner's in New Orleans. Diagnosed at the time as manic-depressive, the Psychiatrist now claim I was suffering the ill effects of a liquid diet. My personal feeling was that Satan was trying to discourage the Remnant Church from deep reconciliation and the Sacrament of Penance due to the outpouring of Divine Mercy.

One of our pious parishioners came in just before my retreat to tell me that Our Lady asked her to warn me, in March; which she failed to do. The warning can be found in the *Apostolate of Holy Motherhood*, March 10. "In regard to Father, I know that he is having many difficulties now, but he must not let these stand in the way of my mission to which I am entrusting to him."(4) Another parishioner at the time I was in the hospital was told by Padre Pio don't worry, Father is OK.

A few days before my departure Alan Fries (the man who sees Angels at St. Margaret Mary) told me how ecstatic my Guardian Angel was over this retreat. "I wish he would tell me," I said.

YOUR GIFT

I have enclosed a picture of Padre Pio in this letter, with a small relic. Padre Pio bore the bleeding wounds of Jesus Christ called the stigmata for 50 years. Because he bled profusely from the wounds when he offered mass, he used modified gloves that became saturated with blood during mass. The blood symbolizes the blood of Christ. Since Padre Pio ate sparingly, some of this blood might have been the blood of Christ.

I was privileged to bless each of your relics with the blood of Padre Pio, which is contained on a glove now kept at San Giovanni. My prayer for each of you is that this holy picture will always remind you that each of us is called to suffer with Jesus Christ. Padre Pio had a ministry of suffering which he carried most of his life.

It is my hope that this relic of Padre Pio also will remind you of the importance of prayer. I have often been discouraged that I pray so poorly. I feel like a mumbler who hurries through my breviary and rosary.

I asked Our Lady why some of us pray so poorly. The answer I was given on the retreat was this: "Prayer is a gift. Ask the heavenly Father for this gift: 'Father I am blind, let me see.' He will give you the gift of prayer."

I also asked for the gift for us to carry our crosses. We are now being asked in this day, that we suffer for the church: St Paul wrote: "...You must make up what is lacking in the sufferings of Jesus Christ".

THE RETREAT

Although I certainly wanted to be cured of my shame, I believe the desire to be healed of my blindness was the chief reason I went to San Giovanni. Since I was 23 years old I have been blind in my right eye. It is difficult for me to read, which I really enjoy. But Our Lady wanted me to learn to suffer willingly.

"Why am I here?" I asked, and Our Lady answered through the graces of the retreat.

Fr. Bush S.J. gave us a wonderful retreat focused on prayer. Fr. Bush and Kathleen Keefe showed us the weapons to use in the battle with the evil one, Satan, the accuser. Fr. Bush works with survivors of child abuse and also priests involved in this terrible crime. He is currently stationed at the Jesuit retreat center at Los Altos, California. Kathleen Keefe has the gift of infused discernment of spirits among her many gifts. She is a wife and mother of seven children in Yonkers, New York.

The priests learned in the retreat about inner healing and praying to overcome Satan in his many diabolical forms. We prayed over each other and shared hours of prayer.

After being prayed over by Fr. Bush and Kathleen, I was told to read St. John's Gospel Chapter 9. This is the same Gospel about the healing of the blind man that changed my life in March. I believe that the result of this prayer has been the healing of my spiritual blindness through Divine Mercy. I pray that I will never again be ashamed to be a priest. I pray that I will be allowed under the cross next to Our Lady at Calvary. I ask you my beloved children to join in the prayer I say nightly. "Lord if there is only one priest left under the cross during the time of chastisement, let it be me".

The most dramatic part of the retreat took place on Sunday. The final talk was given by Kathleen. It was about Our Lady in the upper room awaiting the coming of the Holy Spirit. The priests were moved to tears. In the time of meditation following the talk, I had a clear sense of being with Our Blessed Mother and the other apostles in that upper room.

Initially they were frightened, after all Jesus

had been put to death. Perhaps the Jewish leaders would search out his followers. Fear sent a cold chill through everyone. It almost seemed as if Satan had won.

We know the Blessed Mother was present with the apostles. I imagined Our Blessed Mother telling these frightened priests, "there is good news and bad news", Mary said, "which do you want to hear first?" When you are scared you want to hear the good firSt. "The Holy Spirit will come soon, just as Jesus promised" Our Lady said. "You will all receive special gifts from the Holy Spirit for your ministry."

"The bad news is this...Each of you priests will suffer and die for my Son. But I promise you, I will be at your side. If Mary is with us, we have nothing to fear I thought. Dying for Jesus will be a joy."

This meditation filled me with a great sense of peace. If Mary is with her priest sons, fear will not conquer us.

The retreat ended quietly on Sunday. We were supposed to go to Monte Cassino the next morning. The bus was nearly three hours late. Our Lady had other plans for us. The entire group went back to Padre Pio's tomb to say Mass in the church of Our Lady of Grace. It was the feast of St. James, one of the twelve apostles who was martyred.

After communion Kathleen announced that she had been given a prophesy as well as a mental image of the priests around the altar concelebrating Mass. Each one wore a red stole "I saw your red stoles merge into a gushing river of blood. The blood flowed from the tomb of Padre Pio to Rome where it covered the dome of St. Peter's. _You will suffer martyrdom and some of you will_ *shed your blood,'"* Kathleen said. Instead of being frightened, it only confirmed a sense I had in the meditation from Sunday. We are being called in a special way by Our Lady.

After communion Father James Dressman S.J., the celebrant of the mass, saw an interesting phenomenon. "I saw a white dove with wings extended and the feet visible with red rays emanating from the dove towards the congregation. I take this as a confirmation of the prophesy," Father said. "Was this the Holy Spirit?" I asked myself.

Following the conclusion of Mass an Italian woman came up to Kathleen. This lady is involved in priestly renewal in Milan. "I was given the same exact prophesy for Italian priests", she said, "many priests will shed their blood." Not only was this a confirmation for the American priests but it also made clear the connection between the blood shed by Padre Pio as a "living crucifix" and the call for priests to embrace the cross and allegiance to the Vicar of Christ on earth. Clearly, the Lord set up the itinerary as we traveled to Rome where we concelebrated Mass the following morning at the tomb of St. Peter, apostle, martyr and first Vicar of Christ on earth.

I have never been one to put much stock in dreams. But I would like to share with you the dream I had on Monday night after we reached Rome. In the dream I was awakened by an angel who called my name..."Father Carroll". I sensed it was my Guardian Angel. The angel reached over and put a crown on my head. When I awoke my prayer was: "O, Lord let it be a crown of martyrdom."

I am now reminded of a prophesy that Marija,

one of the visionaries from Medjugorje gave to the priests last year in Baton Rouge. She told us: "persecution will come to the Church in the United States."

My dearest children, Padre Pio should be a reminder to us of the need for prayer and suffering in our lives. We are privileged to live in an age of Divine Mercy. This outpouring of grace will result in the conversion of a multitude of people. We have been told by Our Lady through countless sources that God's wrath can be averted through prayer and fasting.

Tuesday was the feast of St Anne and Joachim, the mother and father of Our Blessed Mother. The prayer of the church on that day in the breviary was this: "God sees all men as sinners, that He might save them."

Each of us in our own way must go to our heavenly Father and tell him of our blindness. "Father I am blind, please let me see." If we do we will experience a tremendous outpouring of Divine Mercy.

It is all about Divine Mercy. I believe the retreat for priests in an Giovanni Rotondo was a plea from Our Lady for repentance. We will experience Divine Mercy once we call upon the Father to heal our blindness. We will see our sinfulness and understand the need for Divine Mercy. But that gift will come only through prayer and suffering.

On Saturday, July 30th I shared my journey at the 6:00 p.m. Mass. One woman coming out of church asked if I had smelt the unusual fragrant odor. "No I had not", I replied. I learned later at my Teams of Our Lady meeting that night that

Padre Pio often makes his presence known through unusual odors.

A prayerful young woman named Lisa stopped after that mass to speak to me. Father, I saw Jesus at mass tonight. She meticulously explained his appearance. At the offertory he appeared behind the altar looking quite sad. "The crown of thorns were evident. Jesus looked so sad," she said, "I couldn't stop crying." "After communion I looked again and this time Jesus was present looking up to heaven."

It is my feeling that this was a confirmation not only of the importance of Divine Mercy in the Remnant Church but also of the renewal of the priesthood as witnessed in the life of Padre Pio, victim priest and "living crucifix". I had wished that through the intercession of Padre Pio I would have been given the gift of sight in my right eye. But I was not. I was given a greater gift, the gift of healing my shame over the priesthood. I have never been more proud of being a Catholic priest. With the grace of the Holy Spirit and the love of Our Blessed Mother, I would gladly be a witness to my love of Jesus Christ and his priesthood, even if it meant the shedding of my blood.

*Editors Note: Kathleen Keefe is the founder of "Peace through Divine Mercy" apostolate for the renewal of the priesthood and the renewal of families. It was through the inspiration given to Kathleen that the retreat for priests was held in San Giovanni Rotondo. I asked Kathleen to share with you some of her insights into this ministry.

THE RETREAT(5)

First Divine Mercy Priests' Retreat
San Giovanni Rotondo, Italy
July 17-27, 1994
"Heal the shepherd - Heal the Flock"
By: Kathleen Keefe

"He said to them, "Come by yourselves to an out-of- the-way place and rest a little." The Gospel of Mark 6:31

The Scripture readings on July 17th of this year had special significance to a group of American priests attending the first "Divine Mercy Priests' retreat" in Italy. Traveling to the peaceful setting of San Giovanni Rotondo in the Gargano mountains, they experienced the power of the word of God to heal hearts and renew spirits.

As co-director of the retreat, I share my reflections from the very privileged vantage point of a laywoman called to establish a retreat ministry to priests during a period of the extraordinary outpouring of Divine Mercy. The prophetic aspect of this ministry is very much in keeping with the prophetic task Jesus has given the church in its mission to preach and teach the gospel. Padre Pio's life exemplifies the call of the Master to proclaim the good news in this Apocalyptic Age. What better place to begin our journey.

Priest as Pilgrim

Why go to San Giovanni Rotondo on retreat? It is precisely the role of **pilgrim** that brings one in touch with the reality **that we are a pilgrim people** on a journey to eternal life. Freely, we choose to leave behind home, family, and those dear to us. Security and comfort become vague memories.

Crossing the Atlantic, sacrificing sleep, and perhaps vacation time, we embrace fatigue and inconvenience, language barriers, and strangers who become appointed companions on the journey. Like dependent children, we rely on our Father to direct and renew us in a manner known only to Him.

Journeying to San Giovanni Rotondo as a pilgrim **restores one's sense of the sacred**. Leaving behind the world of our experience, we focus on the supernatural revealed in and through the life of Padre Pio. In a setting ordained by the master planner, we don't overlook the role of the great St. Michael the Archangel, who graced this region with his appearance some 1500 years before.

A blessed time of the **call to sacrifice** everything (including the financial burden it may entail), we say: "Lord, I come that I might be healed and renewed. Imbue in me the spirit of Padre Pio, your victim priest who willingly embraced the cross, bearing your wounds before the world as 'a living crucifix.'"

It is pure gift offered by God to His priests!

Priest as Penitent

The first recorded statement of Jesus' public ministry was: **"This is the time of fulfillment. The reign of God is at hand! Reform your lives and believe in the gospel!"** (The Gospel of Mark 1:15) It is in repenting of our sins that we reject evil and embrace God. Without true repentance, there can be no genuine surrender to God. Without surrender there is no healing. It is a contrite heart that is healed. The psalmist says: **"My sacrifice, O God, is a contrite spirit; a heart contrite and humbled, O God, you will not spurn."** Psalm 51:19

It is in the silence of retreat from the world that we are free to open ourselves to the grace to experience revulsion at having offended God. In this experience is that encounter with Divine Mercy which Jesus expressed to Blessed Faustina: **"Every time you go to confession, immerse yourself entirely in My mercy with great trust, so that I may pour the bounty of My grace upon your soul. When you approach the confessional, know this, that I myself am waiting there for you. I am only hidden by the priest, but I myself act in your soul. Here the misery of the soul meets the God of mercy."**(6)

The priest as penitent encounters Christ in the model of the humble friar whose zeal for souls was so great that he asked God "to pour out on me the punishments prepared for sinners and for the souls in a state of purgation, even increasing them a hundredfold ..." But it is the priest as penitent encountering Christ in the confessional, through the ministry of his brother priest, that draws him into that deeper conversion that convicts his spirit anew that it truly *is* Christ waiting there for him.

At San Giovanni Rotondo the priest is graced to witness the sign of conversion in the endless lines of repentant sinners. He can now look at empty confessionals and know that it is not a reflection of the ineffectiveness of the priesthood but rather man's loss of the sense of sin and his failure to see through spiritual eyes the healing power in this great sacrament of mercy.

The humble friar continues to call lost sheep to the fold through the Sacrament of Reconciliation as well as be present to his brother priests to remind them of their need to be healed through repentance. This encounter with mercy empowers the priest to call back the lost sheep to the fold. Healing the flock is the natural outgrowth of the priest penitent who has been healed.

Priest as Partner with Christ

The priest as partner with Christ has the unique privilege of calling down on the altar Christ the Victim who offers Himself to the Father in the mystery of the Mass. As partner, the priest shares in the very essence of Christ's life and mission. Renewal of the priest heightens our awareness of Christ's presence in the person of the priest, and releases the fullness of the Spirit of Christ in our midSt. This outpouring of Divine Mercy through the priest is manifested in power through teaching, preaching, healing, miracles and the compassionate love and mercy that pours out of the priest who is truly a partner with Christ. Like Jesus the priest who is healed and renewed " ... calls his own by name and leads them out. When he has brought out [all] those that are his, he walks in front of them, and the sheep follow him because they recognize his voice." The Gospel of John 10:3-4

This partnership is reflected in the mysterious brotherhood that exists when priests are drawn together in the worship of God, the sharing of the joy of ministering to one another, the grace of confessing to each other, the fellowship of love lived out for a higher purpose - that of total surrender to the martyrdom that comes from being the ultimate sign of contradiction in the world.

This was Padre Pio's gift to God and to his fellow man. It was a special gift to his brother priests who assisted and ministered to him through his living crucifixion. This model of unconditional love is the mysterious gift offered to priests today when they respond to Jesus' invitation: **"Let us go off by ourselves to some place where we will be alone and you can rest awhile."**

The Seed Is Planted

Just prior to going to Medjugorje in March, 1987, I met a woman in New York who had been a close friend of Padre Pio's. She invited me to bless myself with a relic containing the still fresh blood from the stigmata of Padre Pio. "One day," she said, "you will understand the importance of Padre Pio in your life and work." Because I had no particular devotion to Padre Pio, I simply thanked her. However, I never forgot her words nor was I ever free of the gnawing question, *"Why Padre Pio?"*

As the Lord prepared me through the years for what would become a public ministry of teaching and healing, my life was immersed in The Divine Mercy. It was clear that the renewal of the priesthood and the renewal of families would be accomplished through God' mercy. I became deeply involved in the spirituality of Sister Faustina and the message Jesus had imparted to this simple Polish sister who died in 1938 at the young age of 33.

Padre Pio and Blessed Faustina

When I had the opportunity to organize a pilgrimage to the beatification of Blessed Faustina I knew I had to go to San Giovanni Rotondo in search of the answer to the mystery of, *"Why Padre Pio?"* Through my work with priests, the connection was now more obvious, but I still didn't know how Padre Pio fit into my life and work. The prophetic words of the woman spoken in New York in 1987 would be the catalyst to lead me to the Gargano Mountains and the unfolding of a great work of God's mercy.

We conducted a healing service in the old church the evening of our arrival. Five priests were present when a prophesy revealed that priests would come from all over the world to San Giovanni Rotondo, a worldwide center for the renewal of the priesthood. Not surprisingly, the five priests present felt called in some way to work for priestly renewal. Three of the five priests attended the first retreat.

A Place of Healing

Something else happened that evening. Many people began to gather in the rear of the church during the healing service. They appeared to be fearful about asking for healing prayer until our seven year old daughter, Kathleen, came for prayer. The sight of a little child gave courage to those in the rear of the church as they came forward for prayer. There was deep conversion and healing that evening. The lord was clearly speaking to us in the healing He was pouring out on those who called on His mercy at the Church of Our Lady of Grace - in the very place where Padre Pio lived out the passion of Christ.

The Retreat Ministry is Born

The following morning as our group boarded the bus for Rome and the beatification of Blessed Faustina, I met Father Joseph at the tomb of Padre Pio for a final prayer. It was bittersweet; I didn't want to leave this place of untold graces and blessings. And so it was in the course of prayer at the tomb that the retreat ministry for priests was born. It was April 17, 1993, the eve of the beatification of the "Secretary of Divine Mercy," Sister Faustina. Thus, the name "Divine Mercy Priests' Retreats." The following day as Pope John Paul, II gave the Body and Blood of Jesus to our seven-year-old daughter, Kathleen, I gazed up at the banner of Blessed Faustina and understood this mission of renewal entrusted to me at the tomb of Padre Pio - a gift of God's mercy!

The Blood of Martyrs

Returning to New York on Holy Saturday, I prayed in earnest in the months that followed. Nothing came to me. In July, I spent four days at the convent of Blessed Faustina and three days traveling throughout Poland with friends. Everywhere we saw the grim reminders of the suffering and persecution endured by a people who would not deny their God nor waver in their love of Mary. Traveling to the Shrine of Our Lady of Lichen, we discovered a jewel in the crown of Poland. For it was here that Mary had given so many messages to her priests. I understood, then, the importance of placing those messages in the heart of Mary's sons. **We are in a special period of healing and mercy for priests. They must come now to Jesus through Mary to be restored to the first fervor of their priesthood.** From Lichen, we went to Warsaw where we visited the church where the memorial is built to Fr. Jerzy Popieluszko, the Solidarity priest brutally murdered for preaching the gospel. At Auchwicz we prayed at the site where St. Maximilian Kolbe received the fatal injection that earned him the crown of martyrdom. At every turn, the power of the priesthood was evident in the shed blood of martyrs, many of them priests and Bishops. Seminaries were overflowing; we met spirit filled priests everywhere. The message was clear.

By December of 1993, I knew the time was approaching to return to Italy. The only word that came in prayer was "March 25th." On the Feast of the Annunciation, I rang the doorbell at the friary of Padre Pio greeting the friar with the words "Padre Giuseppe Pio," almost the full extent of my

Italian. In the days that followed, Father and I were clay in the hands of the potter. The doors opened quickly. The direction of the retreats was clarified during that week as Father and I witnessed many people healed and set free from the power of Satan. Thus, the theme, "Heal the Shepherd, Heal the Flock," was the natural outgrowth of prayer and works of mercy towards suffering souls. Priest as pilgrim, priest as penitent, priest as partner with Christ was undoubtedly the orchestration of Padre Pio establishing the foundation of the ministry in a manner to which he was very accustomed.

Leaders and Martyrs

God is calling forth leaders and martyrs in these times. These leaders and martyrs will be powerful instruments in laying the foundation for the work of renewal. Nowhere was this more evident than at the priests' retreat. As each of the priests embraced the cross and suffering in the spirit of Padre Pio, it was clear that many priests are being called to martyrdom and that some will shed their blood. But the gifts of leadership and martyrdom are never exercised in isolation. God calls forth leaders and martyrs and it is their "yes" that prepares the soil for the renewal of the church. And so it has always been.

The Lesson

Suffering cannot be separated from renewal. They go hand in hand. In the midst of humiliation, stripping, and desolation, we become aware of our own sinfulness and weaknesses. In very mystical ways, the power of suffering frees souls from bondage; the joy of humiliation unites us to the cross; the absolute emptiness of seeking relief from any cross unless that relief is found in the arms of the crucified Savior and the sorrowful Mother becomes clear. Only in surrender of our will to the Divine Will is God's work accomplished. This is the work of renewal and most especially it is the work of the Retreat Ministry.

Rome - The Eternal City

The closing Mass at the tomb of Padre Pio was on the feast of St. James, apostle and martyr. As the priests gathered around the altar facing the tomb of the priest who lived out a unique martyrdom in our times, their stoles appeared to merge into an ocean of red, symbolic of the blood of martyrs bringing life and renewal to the church.

From that holy spot, the priests set out for Rome. The following morning found them at the Tomb of St. Peter where Mass was celebrated. A vivid reminder of the words of Jesus to the first Vicar of Christ on earth: **"I for my part declare to you, you are 'Rock,' and on this rock I will build my church, and the jaws of death shall not prevail against it."** (The Gospel of Matthew 16:18)

Peter, the only disciple personally restored by the Lord, is the great witness to the love and mercy of Jesus towards all of us but especially towards His priests. Three times the Lord asked Peter to declare his love as He entrusted him with the lambs and sheep.

Jesus said to him, **"I tell you solemnly: as a young man you fastened your belt and went about as you pleased; but when you are older you will stretch out your hands, and another will tie you fast and carry you off against your will."** Then Jesus said to him, **"Follow me."** (The Gospel of John 21:18)

"Rebuild My Church" Lay Retreat Ministry

The Lord calls all of us to follow Him. A great blessing that has evolved out of the first priests' retreat is the founding of a retreat ministry for laity called "Rebuild My Church." The first apostles of mercy and renewal will journey to San Giovanni Rotondo in May, 1995 for a three day silent retreat modeled on the priest's retreats. In Rome, they will renew their commitment to the Vicar of Christ and to the magisterium. The journey will culminate in Assisi, where, imbued with the spirit of Francis and Clare, they will continue their formation as apostles of mercy and renewal. The Franciscan Friars of the Renewal will co-direct the retreats with me. Fr. Joseph Pius will assist us as only he can in his tireless work with God's pilgrim people. Fr. Glen Sudano, C.F.R. will open the lay retreat ministry.

The first lay retreat will depart from New York on May 3, 1995 and the second retreat is scheduled to depart on May 17th from New York. The retreats will be a total of ten days including travel. The priests' retreats are scheduled for departure from New York on April 24th and October 9, 1995. Fr. James Dressman, S.J. will co-direct the April retreat for priests. Follow-up programs for both priests' and lay retreat programs will be held at retreat centers in New York, California, Ohio and Louisiana. Additional centers will be established as the program grows.

****

CONCLUSION

We have seen that every Catholic Parish is called to be a Remnant Church. The age of apostasy is fast coming to an end. Each of us must be concerned at the warning Jesus gave us: "When the Son of Man comes, will he find any faith whatsoever?"

We learned through Father Gobbi that we are already in the time of tribulation. (Jan 1, 1993.) We believe that Revelation 12 will occur in our lifetime, Our Blessed Mother will be used by Jesus Christ to overcome Satan. Mary has promised an era of peace after the great battle.

I suspect that this battle has been going on for some time now. From June 18, 1961 to February 13, 1966 Our Lady appeared to children in Garabandal, Spain. The first message, July 4, 1961 said: "We must make many sacrifices, perform much penance and visit the Blessed Sacrament frequently. But first, we must lead good lives. If we do not, a chastisement will befall us. The cup is already filling up and if we do not change, a very great chastisement will come upon us." The second message on June 18, 1965 was more ominous: "As my message of October 18 has not been complied with and as it has not been made known to the world, I am advising you that this is the last one. Before the cup was filling up. Now it is flowing over. Many priests are on the road to perdition and are taking many souls with them. Less and less importance is being given to the Eucharist. You should turn the wrath of God away from yourselves by your efforts. If you ask his forgiveness with sincere hearts, he will pardon you. I, your Mother, through the intercession of St. Michael the Archangel, wish to tell you that you should make amends. You are now receiving the last warnings. I love you very much and do not want you condemned. You should make more sacrifices. Reflect on the passion of Jesus."

I had the opportunity to speak extensively with

Dick Polak from Denver, Colorado. Dick has worked for nearly twenty years spreading the message of Garabandal. He has been favored by the Lord with great insight and blessings.

Dick confirmed what I had read, that Padre Pio had a deep belief in the apparitions at Garabandal. This clearly renewed my interest in these apparitions since I have rediscovered Padre Pio. Dick also told me that Padre Pio had sent a letter to Conchita, one of the visionaries. She immediately got an answer from Our Lady for Padre Pio.

According to Dick, it was Padre Pio who sent Joey Limongina to Garabandal. Joey is a blind man who has been a major instrument in the spread of the messages of Garabandal.

Apparently Padre Pio had a vision before his death of the great miracle spoken of in Garabandal as well as other apparition sites. Because of the interest of Padre Pio, I am much more inclined to accept the authenticity of these visions despite the fact that the Church has not ruled on them.

In the pamphlet entitled "The Warning" by Father Philip Bebie, C.P. we can get an insight into things that will probably occur shortly.

APPARITIONS AT GARABANDAL

Certain things stand out at Garabandal that can be found in many of Our Lady's messages around the world.

1. <u>The Warning</u>. Apparently everyone will be given the grace to see themselves as they are. I believe this was the gift that I received in early March, 1994. It is all about Divine Mercy...not fear or anxiety.

2. <u>The Miracle</u>. This great miracle will result in the conversion of many. This has also been prophesied by Our Lady at Medjugorje and elsewhere.
3. The Punishment (chastisement). The children at Garabandal were told that if people did not convert after the miracle, a great punishment would ensue.

At Fatima in 1917 Our Lady indicated that there would be a Triumph of the Immaculate Heart of Mary and then an era of Peace.

THE WARNING

Fr. Bebie, C.P. was dying from cancer. He had entrusted a small manuscript, entitled "The Warning" to a friend to be published after the warning occured. According to Our Blessed Mother, she told the children in Garabandal, Spain that she had obtained the warning to help make it possible for the world to avoid the chastisement. Our Lady had already promised at Fatima in 1917 that, "Russia would be converted and the triumph of the Immaculate Heart would occur and an era of peace would be granted to mankind."

Because of fear that many would reject the "warning" out of ignorance, it was decided to publish Fr. Bebie's manuscript. Perhaps it would help if more people understood the message given at Garabandal, by Our Lady. Fr. Bebie died in 1986, the same year that his work was printed. It is clear from this pamphlet that the "warning" will be an act of Divine Mercy.

According to Fr. Bebie, Blessed Anna Maria Tiagi spoke of a great chastisement that would come upon the world. However, proceeding this chastisement she said there would be an illumination of conscience. Everyone would see themselves as God sees them. According to Blessed Anna Maria this miracle of self illumination called "the warning" would result in many individuals being saved. Blessed Anna Maria Tiagi was beatified in 1920. She was considered not only a prophetess, but a great mystic.

St. John Bosco, whose vision of the "end times" can be found on the back cover of this book, was told by Our Lady that she would obtain a victory for Christianity before the year 2,000. It would be a greater victory for Christianity than Lepanto. The victory of Lepanto turned away the Turks in their efforts to overrun Christianity in Europe.

According to the prediction of Our Lady at Garabandal, the great miracle would occur within a year of "the warning". This warning is meant to be a time of grace to see yourself as you are. It is an act of Divine Mercy.

The warning will be given to everyone as a sign of the future. It will prepare us for the miracle promised not only at Garabandal but Medjugorje as well. It is a time of choice. Choose God or Satan.

As I read this small work, "The Warning", I was struck by the similarities to the experience I had in March, 1994. I believe the grace I received at that time was the gift of illumination, which Our Lady called "the warning" at Garabandal. I came to understand the meaning of Divine Mercy. When I read Fr. Bebie's it made clear to me that perhaps I was given a foretaste of the "warning". According to Fr. Bebie the warning will be given to everyone as a sign of the future. It will prepare us for the great miracle.

Fr. Bebie wrote, "the warning is the first worldwide intervention in history in which God directly warns each of us of a final and eternal punishment to come if we do not repent of our sins."

THE MIRACLE

It finally became clear to me why it is so important for all of us to understand the warning. Our Lady was reported to have said at Garabandal that if we truly repent after receiving the warning, we can avert the chastisement or at least lessen it's impact. At Garabandal the children were told that following the warning a great miracle would be visible to the world. This sign will be Eucharistic as well as Marian. It is possible that this miracle will be the cause of the world converting to Jesus Christ. Understanding the warning will help us to prepare for the miracle that might usher in world conversion to Jesus Christ.

THE PUNISHMENT

According to Our Lady at Garabandal, the punishment or chastisement will take place after the miracle, if the world does not repent. It will purify the earth. It will not be the end of the world, nor will it be a war.

The children at Garabandal had a foretaste of this punishment during the Novena for Corpus Christi in 1962. The four children were left alone in the darkness outside the village. They were told to instruct the people not to follow them. The villagers heard the children screaming in terror. When the people prayed the wailing stopped but continued when their prayers ceased.

The four had witnessed the punishment. They were told the punishment would happen if mankind doesn't amend it's ways. Mari Loli, one of the four visionaries, told of fire over all the world. Even the sea was on fire and there was nowhere to flee.

A Permanent Sign

The children at Garabandal were told that a permanent sign would remain at the pines until the end of the world. Our Lady promised that this sign would be a call to holiness. It will point us to heaven. This sign will be able to be seen and televised.

The Triumph

At Fatima, Our Lady spoke of the Triumph of the Immaculate Heart of Mary. It is the plan of Jesus Christ that his mother will crush the head of Satan.

Revelation 12 is part of this promise. Because of the triumph of the Immaculate Heart of Mary, an era of peace will be given to the world. The Remnant Church is a story of Divine Mercy. I believe that the Holy Spirit has prepared many Catholic communities to survive the coming trials.

Why Should We Accept the Message of Garabandal?

It is true that despite six church commissions, the apparitions of Garabandal have not been approved by the Church. In the seventh commission we were told that approval would not be given until the fulfillment of the "warning" as well as the "miracle."

Since these apparitions will not be approved until it is too late to do any good, Fr. Bebie decided to print his small work, "The Warning."

Frankly, I was quite resistant to publishing a revised edition (third printing) of the "Remnant Church". I felt I had done what Our Lady wanted me to do; to let everyone know the importance in our day of Eucharistic Adoration, love of Our Lady and loyalty to the Holy Father.

I had swallowed my pride and told my parishioners that the alleged apparitions of Theresa Lopez were declared "not of supernatural origin", by the church commission.

But Our Lady once again led me to revise the "Remnant Church. She allowed me to experience Divine Mercy. And when I failed to understand the experience she gave me two signs. One was the small pamphlet of Fr. Bebie called "The Warning". The other was the priest retreat at San Giovanni and the exposure to the gifts of Kathleen Keefe which is closely related to Divine Mercy.

I knew in my heart that the prophesy that American priests would suffer was authentic. I had heard this prophesy given first by Marija, a visionary from Medjugorje, to priests in Baton Rouge, Louisiana. This was similar to the message given to Kathleen Keefe in San Giovanni. Some priests will be called upon to give up their lives.

What right do I have to keep silent? The message I bring you is the enormity of Divine Mercy.

Perhaps we can learn a lesson from history. When Eastern Europe was being systematically destroyed by Hitler and Stalin, two cities were left untouched, Cracow, Poland and Vilno, Lithuania.

These two cities were the center of Divine Mercy. Will God spare the Remnant Church that allow themselves to be open to Divine Mercy? This is certainly my prayer.

I cannot guarantee that in a future time the church may rule that Garabandal is not of supernatural origin. But I can promise you this, if you personally experience Divine Mercy, you will do everything in your power to tell the world of the great love of Jesus Christ through his Divine Mercy.

Healing?

Are there any other elements to be found in the Remnant Church besides love of the Eucharist, devotion to Our Lady, loyalty to the Pope and openness to Divine Mercy?

I feel in my heart that the Holy Spirit will give the remnant signs involving Eucharistic healing. Many of us have seen some of the gifts of the Holy Spirit in healing services. The grip of Satan is often loosened and spiritual healing frequently occur. When physical healing begins to take place regularly, I suspect that the "warning" is near.

Our Lady has implored her children to pray especially for priests. I would like to be a small channel used by her to your hearts that you heed her plea. Pray for Priests.

Conclusion

A parishioner recently shared a number of visions she had in St. Margaret Mary. She saw the Heart of Jesus as pictured in Divine Mercy, pulsating with love for each of us. She saw the grace of the Holy Spirit falling on the heads of many individuals on Pentecost. Some seemed to hold a cover, like a newspaper over their heads. "What is the meaning of this," she asked?

"Most of the parishioners are receiving the Holy Spirit." She was told. But many cover their heads and prevent his grace from coming. They have their own agenda.

This woman also saw the bubble covering the community. She knew it was the protection of Our Lady over the Remnant Church. The bubble was similar to a tent. "Prepare to accept many many more," she was told.

I believe Jesus is coming again ... not as a child ... but in his Divine Mercy. "Come Lord Jesus, Come! "

The End Times

I am sure when many of our readers heard that Pope John Paul II had said in a sermon that we live in the end times they were frightened. It is clear that he did not mean the end of the world, but rather that our world will be completely different when the Messiah returns again.

One of our prayerful women was given a beautiful passage in scripture to read, to help myself and others focus on the good news that you will live to see, in the era of peace. These words can be found in the Book of Tobit beginning at Chapter 13.

These are the salient passages:

Divine Mercy

"He scourged you for your iniquities, but will again

have _mercy_ on you all." Tobit 13:5

"Turn back, you sinner! do the right before him: perhaps he may look with favor upon you and show you mercy."
Tobit 13:6

The Power Of Repentance

"When you turn back to him with all your heart, to do what is right before him, Then he will turn back to you, and no longer hide his face from you." Tobit 13:6

Jesus King Of Men And Angels

"Bless the Lord of righteousness and exalt the King of the ages." Tobit 13:6

The Righteous (Good) Have Nothing To Fear During The Time Of The Chastisements.

"Go then, rejoice over the children of the righteous, ... Happy are all the men who shall grieve over you, over all your _chastisements_, For they shall rejoice in you as they behold all your joy forever." Tobit 13:13

It Will Only Be A Remnant That Will Survive.

"Jerusalem shall be rebuilt ... Happy for me if a remnant of my offspring survive." Tobit 13:16.

It Will Be A Time Of Divine Mercy.

"God's temple there shall be burnt to the ground

and shall be desolate for a while. But God will again have mercy on them and bring them back to the land of Israel."
Tobit 14:4-5.

It Will Be A Time Of Evangelization. Conversion To The Catholic Church Will Be A Sign Of The True Church.

"They shall rebuild the temple, but it will not be like the first one, until the era when the appointed times shall be completed." Tobit 14:5

The Era Of Peace Will Be A Time Of Great Joy To The World.

"Afterward all of them shall return from their exile, and they shall rebuild Jerusalem with splendor." Tobit 14:5.

It Will Be A Time Of Universal Conversion.

"All the nations of the world shall be converted and shall offer God true worship;" Tobit 14:6.

"... all shall abandon their idols which have deceitfully led them into error, ..." Tobit 14:6.

What a magnificent picture of the era of peace. The world will be converted and peace will reign. The dream was sketched out by Our Lady all the way back at Fatima in 1917. The third secret of Fatima - Apostasy of Clergy and Laity is nearly over. The time for peace is soon at hand. There are battles left to fought. But Mary will crush the head of the serpent with the help of Michael the Archangel. And Jesus will return in glory.

I learned of a parishioner who was in prayer in our chapel recently. During his time of adoration, beautiful light beams began to come from a picture of Divine Mercy. He was so intrigued he got up to look at the picture. But there was no picture. It had been moved to the main church. I feel that is a confirmation that we are in a period of Divine Mercy.

I would urge each of you to work to bring about the Triumph of the Immaculate Heart of Mary and the return of Jesus Christ in glory. But each of us must begin with ourselves. Divine Mercy is not possible without repentance.

The role of the remnant church is clear ... love of Christ present in the Eucharist, devotion to Our Blessed Mother and loyalty to the Pope and the Church. But for each of us it begins with repentance, so that we can receive Divine Mercy. If enough people repent we will be spared the worst of the tribulations.

The triumph of the Immaculate Heart of Mary will usher in the final coming of Jesus Christ in glory. That is the dream Our Lady has put into our hearts, to prepare for the coming of the Lord. We end with the final words of scripture, "... Come, Lord Jesus!"

[1]Sister M. Faustina Kowalska, *Divine Mercy in My Soul: Diary* (Stockbridge, Massachusetts: Marian Press, 1987).

[2]Editors note: Father Ken Harney was an

associate pastor of St. Margaret Mary Church from 1989 to 1993. I feel his story illustrates the incredible mercy of Jesus Christ. Ken served in the Navy for twenty years. As a recovering alcoholic he entered the seminary and was ordained a Catholic priest. In his brief time at St. Margaret Mary he distinguished himself by his love of the Sacrament of Penance and his ability to assist the deeply troubled through counseling. Father Harney was replace in June, 1993 by Fr. Joe Benson. Fr. Joe Benson is also referred to in this chapter as Father Joe.

[3]Archbishop J. Francis Stafford, "Declaration Concerning Alleged Apparitions of the Blessed Virgin Mary at Mother Cabrini Shrine and Other Places in the Archdiocese of Denver" 9 March 1994.

[4]Mark Miravalle, *The Apostolate of Holy Motherhood* (Milford, OH. 45150: The Riehle Foundation, P.O. Box 7, 1991), p. 44.

[5]For Information on the Apostolate or on the retreat program write to:

Mercy Retreats
25 Cambridge Avenue
Yonkers, N.Y. 10707
Phone: (914) 337-0773 or (914) 337-0728

[6]Sister M. Faustina Kowalska, *Divine Mercy in My Soul: Diary* (Stockbridge, Massachusetts: Marian Press, 1987).